From Hellifield
to the Himalaya

Sue Pugh

2QT (Publishing) Ltd

First Edition published 2019 by
2QT Limited (Publishing)
Settle, N. Yorkshire

Publisher Disclaimer:
The events in this memoir are described according to the Author's
recollection; recognition and understanding of the events and
individuals mentioned and are in no way intended to mislead or
offend. As such the Publisher does not hold any responsibility for
any inaccuracies or opinions expressed by the author. Every effort
has been made to acknowledge and gain any permission from
organisations and persons mentioned in this book. Any enquiries
should be directed to the author.

Drawings and illustrations: © Steve Conway - sc-artworks.co.uk
Front cover image: © Martin Moran. Ledge Route, Carn Dearg, Scotland
Back cover image: © Dave Pugh. Pen-y-Ghent, Yorkshire Dales

Printed in Great Britain by TJ International

A CIP catalogue record for this book is available
from the British Library

ISBN 978-1-913071-33-2

Content

INTRODUCTION

A Taste of Things to Come – March 2018

'I HATE TO say this, Dave, but we are going to look pretty ridiculous.' The car was packed with two huge rucksacks, ice axes, crampons, helmets and a rope, not forgetting two pairs of B3 mountaineering boots that should have come with a health warning due to their close similarity to lead-lined boots, both in weight and lack of comfort. For years I was blissfully unaware there were different categories of boots.

It was only a twenty-minute drive to the start of the task that lay ahead of us. We left the comfort of our home in Hellifield; our next stop would be Horton-in-Ribblesdale, a small rural village in the heart of the Yorkshire Dales. This was where we would start the ascent of Pen-y-Ghent, a shapely peak which boasts a height of 694m (2277ft) and forms part of the popular Yorkshire Three Peaks route.

It is not uncommon to hear of people venturing into the hills and mountains unprepared for the terrain or changes in weather they might encounter. However, even those with the most vivid imaginations would have concluded that Dave and I could be classed as 'over the top' with all the gear we were either carrying or wearing. Added to which, the fells were a lovely shade of green and there wasn't a snowflake in sight.

So, had we finally lost our marbles? I like to think not. We were just like any other couple preparing for a forthcoming trip. We had booked to go on an expedition to the Indian Himalaya, hoping to climb a rarely visited peak – providing the authorities and local military would sanction our permits and allow us to enter the area. Should we get the green light, we would probably have the mountain to ourselves.

Pen-y-Ghent featured in our training regime. Admittedly, it didn't spring to mind as being comparable to the Himalaya but we had to practise carrying heavy packs. And the B3 boots desperately needed running in, in the same way that you would 'run in' a new car in days gone by. Remember those stickers in the rear window stating: 'Running in, Please Pass'? From that reference, you'll gather that I'm not in the first flush of youth although I was only a child when such notices could be seen.

Of course, what we were doing made sense... That did little to allay my fears about what others might think of our paraphernalia. It was at times like this that I envied my husband's attitude of 'they can think what they want, I don't care'.

Most of the gear could be hidden away in our rucksacks, with the exception of the axes. It was mid-week so there were fewer people at Horton than on a Saturday, but the chances were still high we would meet somebody along the way.

The car was locked and I reluctantly left the comforting camouflage of Wobble. (Yes, I am one of the many who give their car a name and, as WOB features in the registration, it seemed a natural choice.)

We headed towards Brackenbottom, a popular and attractive route which takes you up what's commonly known as the nose of Pen-y-Ghent. It is the quickest and most direct way to the summit but, on reaching the base of the nose, we took a slight diversion where few people go. It is slightly longer, 'off-piste' and leads to a relatively steep grassy gap. On a busy weekend, when poor old Pen-y-Ghent can be inundated with

'Three Peakers', this is an excellent route to find the peace and solitude the hills have to offer. Apologies, but I shall remain vague and rather selfish as to its whereabouts or it will no longer be a secret. I'm not a lover of these programmes and articles about secret hideaways; how can they possibly remain secret after they've been publicised?

It was possible that the gully might be holding some snow from a few days earlier when there'd been a cold spell and we could play with our axes, but no such luck. Also, the lack of snow made the route anything but pleasurable as our boots were not designed for soft, uneven grass. But at least on our off-piste trail we didn't experience the embarrassment of meeting fellow outdoor enthusiasts...

That was about to change when we reached the trig point. Shuffle as I might, I could not keep my axe on the blind side of the couple we met at the top of the mountain. They didn't say a word, other than passing the time of day, but their stares said it all. Hurriedly we bade them farewell, only to meet up with more people who glanced back at us curiously.

The straw that broke the camel's back was an encounter with a man who commented, 'Do you know something I don't?' There's always one, isn't there? When Dave tried to explain that we'd been in search of snow and we were training for the Himalaya, the man just smiled – or was it a smirk?

Perhaps we seemed unlikely candidates for such a destination. I like to think we are wearing well. Didn't he know that being sixty-plus was the new forty-plus? Better late than never, I say. Mentally I ran through all the clichés, but in truth he was wearing my axe in his head!

My boots were crippling me. What a welcome sight, dear Wobble appearing in the distance.

This Himalaya expedition was testing us – and we were still in Yorkshire...

PART ONE

THE PAST – 2016.

The Party's Over

Midnight Magic

Brief Encounters

007 or 951?

The Party's Over

MINUTES SEEMED LIKE hours as I dialled 999 for a second time. It was the 27th October 1989 and many of the country's labour forces were in the midst of industrial action, including the ambulance service. The army was on standby. At that very moment all I wanted was help from somebody – anybody.

A wonderful ambulance crew attended and promptly radioed for paramedic back-up. Paul had now lost consciousness. For close on an hour they worked on him tirelessly before heading to Bradford Royal Infirmary.

I knew this was serious, and being asked to sit in the front of the ambulance confirmed my thoughts. The crew did not want to risk a wife becoming hysterical in the close confines of an ambulance as they performed CPR on her husband. I could have assured them that I usually stay calm in a crisis, but I fully understood their misgivings.

Paul died that evening. In January 1990, I went to scatter his ashes at sea. The Lizard/Cadgwith lifeboat crew could not have been kinder as they handed me a life-jacket. Paul and I visited Cornwall regularly. The manager of the Polurrian Hotel, where we often stayed, happened to be a crew member of the RNLI lifeboat and was more than willing to help with my request.

Only six weeks prior to Paul's death, we had been on the beach and come across an empty ashes container that had been washed up. I couldn't help thinking that it was regrettable that somebody had died but disappointing that the container had not been disposed of responsibly. As we looked out to sea Paul announced, totally out of the blue, that this was where he would like his ashes scattering. Little did I know that wish would be carried out only weeks after that visit. Even taking into account our age difference, his was still an early and untimely death.

After seven years of wondering what life was all about, a new door to happiness finally opened. I had considered that becoming a nun was an option; alternatively, life would continue being just me and my two dogs, Ben, a golden retriever, and Frank, a border terrier.

In many ways, life with the dogs was a much simpler carry-on; they were always willing to listen, understood me completely and never stood me up. I'd been in search of a new relationship, only to lurch from one disaster to another – until Mr Pugh came on the scene.

There was an instant attraction, even after I wrote a note on a business card that I left on the windscreen of his car. It was probably a surprise to him as I worked in the funeral service at the time! Admittedly, it was a slightly unusual occupation; I left school at the age of sixteen and worked for Barclays Bank. Eight years later Dad died, curiosity got the better of me and I found myself employed in the funeral service.

The dogs approved of Dave, and Dave approved of the dogs. Had Dave failed this test, it would have been curtains to our new relationship. Thankfully 1997 proved to be a major turning point in my life and the start of many amazing adventures and newfound happiness. Adventurous sums up Dave nicely.

From meeting on a walk to moving in with me took all of eight weeks; within twelve months we were married. If at first you don't succeed, or perhaps it was a case of third time lucky as I am Mrs Pugh Version Three. I'm cautiously optimistic about our future as I have lasted twice as long as his previous two wives.

They say that opposites attract and that was certainly the case in the early days. Before meeting Dave, I had a tick list for the man of my dreams. Dave received more crosses than ticks, so I have no idea how he slipped through the net. Perhaps subconsciously I was ready for a challenge. He was the owner of a clapped-out car and a motorbike; he speaks loudly, has little diplomacy, but is soft as putty in the middle. The years have been kind to him as he has obviously mellowed. When I hear of his youth and formative years, I know for a fact he would not have received a solitary tick on my checklist.

It still surprises Dave how naive I was and what a sheltered life I'd led when I was young. He could not believe I had, and never have, witnessed a fight. However, it works both ways; only recently Dave has taken to reading Brontë novels, which is totally out of character. I am by no means a bookworm and I only read *Jane Eyre* in my schooldays when I had to. He loves the Brontës' frequent use of the word 'vexed' so now hardly a day goes by without him using it. I'm as daft, so I love it!

Over a period of time I found myself attempting all manner of things that Dave persuaded me I would enjoy. Had I been a gambler, I would have lost on several occasions. For example, I rode pillion on a super-sports motorbike when I thought I hated them. It was a real buzz with the acceleration, although on one particular day I did question my sanity ...

Dave replaced the back tyre on the bike every six weeks or so; soft compound gives excellent grip but wears extremely quickly. It had been nearly eight weeks, due to a delay with the garage, and the tyre was at its legal limit. Dave suspected a police car was tailing us and feared we would be stopped. No, we didn't foolishly tear off into the distance but we took advantage of the fact that two wheels can get through traffic more easily than four wheels and still remain within the law.

Left, right, right, left; we ended up in a crowded car park. The bike was parked up and I found myself lurking behind some dustbins, checking to see if the coast was clear. This was one time I regretted wearing brightly coloured blue-and-yellow leathers, not the best camouflage! It seems ironic that Dave's son, and several of our friends, are police officers.

Paul had introduced me to walking, a stroll around Bolton Abbey in the Dales progressing to a walk up Catbells, a popular mountain in the Lake District. Now Dave was taking me to a different level on serious, demanding routes in the Lake District before the heady heights of the Highlands. Those of you acquainted with the Scottish mountains will appreciate the seriousness of these ventures. Then I found myself dipping my toes into the world of winter mountaineering. Previously I'd been ignorant of such things as ice axes and crampons, those huge spikey things that explorers wear when they are climbing Everest – but now I was learning.

Dave's outlook on marriage could also be regarded as adventurous. Three weeks before the wedding, I expressed concern as to whether it was the right move. Maybe it was pre-nuptial nerves but I felt I had to forewarn Dave.

'We'll give it a go and I'm sure we'll be fine,' was his reply.

He was right, despite our honeymoon being less than conventional. The Northern Pennines can be bleak at the best of times and November is not the ideal month for good weather. No matter; Dave had a walk that he wanted to try over Cross Fell.

We were having a few days in the Lake District so, according to Dave, it was an excellent opportunity to pop across to the Northern Pennines. We had the place to ourselves, which might be regarded as romantic – but that was where the romance ended. Huddled over a map, the wind blowing, driving rain and visibility more or less zero was less than idyllic.

I asked, 'Are we lost?'

Dave assured me, 'No, just checking exactly where we are!

January 2016. Life as we'd known it for the last three years had ended. The party was over in more ways than one as we left the Ledgowan Lodge Hotel at Achnasheen in the north-west highlands of Scotland.

Perhaps it was my imagination, but Fionn Bheinn looked particularly splendid with the sun shining down on her snow-clad summit. Detail was difficult to distinguish as I tried in vain to fight back the tears of both joy and sadness.

Dave and I had just completed climbing all 282 Munros, most of them within a three-year period. Numerous visits to Scotland and planning which Munros to bag had become an enjoyable obsession and a way of life. Without wishing to teach your grandma how to suck eggs, a very rough description of a Munro is a mountain more than 914.4m (3000 ft) in height. There are some subsidiary tops to mountains which can be of such a height but do not come under the category of a Munro.

Strictly speaking all Scottish mountains, whatever category they fall into, are referred to as hills, but in my eyes they are mountains. As for 'bagging', that's another way to say you are climbing them and ticking them off the list. This is anything but a technical book, so that is where I'll leave it.

Fionn Bheinn was the final Munro, which was bagged on a milestone birthday of mine with eighteen of our friends. We had enjoyed a magical time at Ledgowan, ecstatic at achieving the goal, but there was a sense of emptiness because it had come to an end. What now?

We would happily continue to visit Scotland and promised our friends, who also had been smitten with the Munro-bagging bug, that we would be pleased to accompany them in their quest. But it would not be the same. Admittedly, we could be more selective about which Munros we would re-visit; we'd also make damned sure we were busy when the few Munros you wouldn't wish on your worst enemy appeared on their agenda. There weren't many in that category; time is a great healer and the mind has an uncanny knack of blanking out trauma. In retrospect, sixteen hour days, foul weather, being eaten alive by midges and wading rivers in the pitch black hadn't been that horrendous after all.

As we headed back to Yorkshire, I only had fond memories of my mountains; they had become very special friends of mine and better than any drug a doctor could offer.

They say that as one door closes another one opens and I agree, but that does not come easily to an impatient, self-confessed control freak. The urge to peek through the keyhole of the next potential door often ends in disappointment; we can only dictate to a certain degree what the future may bring. Engineering or plucking another challenge out of thin air would be futile; like it or not, I would have to let life take its course.

Midnight Magic

I THINK I need to introduce you to Martin Moran as his name will crop up several times as I tell my story. Martin is a professional mountain guide based in the north-west of Scotland. He is a highly respected mountaineer with many achievements under his belt, and he's a published author. A down-to-earth character, he strives to offer his clients memorable times in the mountains, taking them to their limits and beyond to achieve experiences that seemed unimaginable. He is a charming man but a hard taskmaster; you'll love him one minute and strike him off your Christmas card list the next, particularly when you find yourself dangling from a rope with your nose pressed against a rock face and all you asked for was an enjoyable day out! However, I would trust Martin with my life; indeed, on several occasions I've done just that.

So, the Munros were bagged, I had no challenges on the horizon so a trip abroad might be just the tonic. Not being a lover of beach holidays or sightseeing tours, Martin's website seemed the ideal place to search for ideas. Like any good website it all looked wonderful, but apprehension set in as I read the detail. It was fine for aspiring mountaineers but sounded totally out of my league and listed destinations such as Norway, the Alps and even the Himalaya.

My mistake was showing Dave, who was like a child in a sweet shop. 'Let's go here, let's go there,' he urged as I was having palpitations and pondering on a large G&T to calm my nerves. I'd been under the impression that booking a holiday was a relaxing and enjoyable experience.

Martin had been my guide when I climbed the Inaccessible Pinnacle on Skye with my friend Anita, and both Dave and I had attended one of Martin's 'easy' winter-mountaineering courses in Scotland. It was an amazing experience but I was decidedly at my limit, so to consider anything more taxing seemed ridiculous.

Normally I am a very decisive person, but when it comes to mountaineering I am my own worst enemy. I believe there are three categories of people: those who definitely want to do something; those who definitely don't, and then there's my category. The thought scares me silly but a little voice in my head is nagging me, saying that I do want to give it a go.

Encouraged by the possibility of seeing the Midnight Sun, I agreed to Norway. Carl, one of our Munro-bagging friends, would join us.

Before I go any further, let me introduce you to Anita and Carl. Anita is a friend I met through walking who I managed to persuade (or perhaps con) that she *would* enjoy climbing the Inaccessible Pinnacle with me in 2012. Dave couldn't join us on the trip; he had already climbed the 'In Pinn', and a husband leading his wife on that route could have led to serious repercussions!

Anita and I remain good friends, despite the In Pinn, and she joined Dave and I on many of our Munro-bagging trips. She has since completed a full round of the Munros. Neither of us could be regarded as naturals when it comes to climbing, but we give it our best shot.

I could learn a lot from Anita, who is streets ahead of me when it comes to tact and diplomacy and plays her cards close to her chest. I wear my heart on my sleeve and will confess all; I offer comprehensive explanations when they are not required without even realising it. Perhaps one day I'll learn how to answer a question with a simple yes or no!

Initially Carl was one of Dave's walking friends in the days when the two of them went away for long weekends on serious walking and climbing trips. That was before the women gatecrashed their forays. He also joined the 'Munro club' and at present is seventy short of completing a full round. He's a very placid, easy-going chap – but God forbid you come between him and his pork pies!

It was an unexpected leisurely first day in Norway, insofar as we missed our connecting flight to Tromsø. Sitting on the hotel terrace on a balmy sunny evening watching the world go by was very relaxing. Had we not been in Norway, with prices that make your eyes water, I think a little more alcohol would have been consumed.

We belatedly met up with Martin at Tromsø airport and had a comparatively short journey, including a ferry crossing, to our accommodation and the nearby Lyngen Alps. The Norwegian weather was reminiscent of Scotland: low cloud with drizzle. One day was spent in the fog floundering in deep snow, but luckily the forecast promised better conditions and the prospect of experiencing the Midnight Sun.

Martin is a great believer in travelling light and fast, so there was just a single, two-man tent and the other two would bivvy (sleep outside). Travelling light was, and still is, an art I need to perfect. Fast is a far more formidable proposition. The trek in to our proposed wild-camping area involved a considerable distance negotiating a large boulder field. I might be 'steady away' on normal terrain but when it comes to boulders, 'steady' takes on a whole new meaning.

To be fair, Martin was very patient and offered words of encouragement with a wry grin on his face. 'Sue, we've only six weeks before it gets dark!' I suppose he thought that was funny ... yes, it was! I would like to point out that there had been a discussion at the outset whether we should take what appeared to be the direct route over the boulders or, as I suggested, aim for the river where we stood a good chance of traversing easier, flatter ground. The men voted for 'direct' but they chose my route on our return.

A suitable site was found to pitch the tent. It was a lunar landscape with an abundance of rock, which would test the comfort of the sleep-mat. There was little greenery but the convenience of a river close at hand. The neighbouring mountains that lined the valley were shrouded in mist although occasionally we caught a glimpse of them.

Dave and I had been offered the tent while Carl and Martin would bivvy. Martin would utilise my new bivvy bag. I was proud of my lightweight bag, knowing weight was often an issue, but unfortunately Martin was less enamoured with my new purchase. 'Sue, this is too flimsy. It's a sleeping bag cover.'

I had bought it online and it definitely mentioned it could be used as a minimalist bivvy. I was still somewhat new to the words 'bivvy bags', let alone their merits. I offered to change places with Martin but he opted to risk test-driving my bag. No problem; he had worried for nothing.

With the weather improving, the plan was to try and sleep in the early evening before setting out in search of the Midnight Sun. Twenty-four-hour daylight played havoc with our body-clocks and minds. Preparing to climb a 500m (1640 ft) snow gully at ten o'clock at night, with the snow sparkling in the sun, was weird yet exciting.

Time was immaterial as we climbed. The views that surrounded us were stunning. The sun reflected off a distant fjord; the surrounding rocks that cocooned us had a warm glow, with different hues of yellow, gold and brown. What a magical reward for the effort of scaling one helluva gully at 1am.

It seems to be a unique area. It is a recognised wilderness and home to glaciers, yet the highest mountain, Jiehkkevárri, is a moderate 1834m (6014ft), only fifty percent larger than Ben Nevis and half the size of the Swiss or French Alps. But the area offers serious routes and climbs and it is not be underestimated. The huge bonus, as far as I was concerned, was the absence of crowds.

Another few minutes and we would be standing on the summit of The Wedding Peak with ample opportunity for a photo shoot – except the mountain had other ideas. The cloud rolled in, a breeze very quickly became a bitingly cold wind, and visibility was sweet Fanny Adams.

The route Martin had in mind for our descent was abandoned as he discovered an alternative, easier escape. I was assured it was only a snowbank at an angle, which could easily be used by skiers, but it looked steep to me; as for having 'two planks of wood' strapped to your feet to negotiate such territory, skiers must be total head cases. Skiing is a dodgy sport and nearly as dodgy as some ski instructors. One of my disastrous relationships in the pre-Mr Pugh era involved a ski instructor, but I'm sure I'll forget it one fine day!

With a determined attitude, we were back on track and heading in the direction of camp. This had now become an endurance test. The magic of the Midnight Sun had disappeared, to be replaced with cloud and drizzle and suddenly, at around 4am, my body objected to the rigours of the day – or rather the night. Not only did we need to walk back to camp but then we had to break camp, pack up and walk out of the wilderness. Our previous Scottish Munro efforts now paid dividends: endurance, acceptance of the situation, and get on with it.

I was fortunately unaware that Dave and Carl experienced underwear issues in Norway. Our cabin was tiny and somehow someone picked up the wrong pair of underpants. Dave realised he'd been wearing Carl's; that was okay but for the fact they were 'used'. They found it hilarious; all I can say is – grim.

Norwegian Fjords and the Midnight Sun

Emerging from the gully

Stunning Lyngen Alps at 1.00am. Five minutes later zero visibility!

Crevasses en route to Allalinhorn

Allalinhorn summit in the distance shrouded in mist

The mighty Matterhorn

Queuing at the base of the Matterhorn

Summit ridge of the Matterhorn

Brief Encounters

TWO MONTHS LATER, Dave and I were heading to Saas Fee in Switzerland for the match between David and Goliath, or rather Dave and the Matterhorn. Only Dave and Martin were climbing the Matterhorn; even Martin, with his optimistic outlook, would not put my name in the same sentence as 'Matterhorn'. Much relieved, I was there to offer support and as a bystander on this challenge.

Several people asked Dave why he chose the Matterhorn when Mont Blanc is the highest mountain in the Alps. From what I've gleaned, the Matterhorn is a far more technical climb and requires more skill. Size isn't everything, and that's very true when it comes to mountains.

I'd never noticed that the symbol on a Toblerone is the Matterhorn; it portrays the archetypal shape and image of a perfect mountain. If you look very carefully, there is a bear in the mountain, which relates to the Swiss town of Bern being 'The City of Bears'. Enough of the trivia: (I like Toblerone, the dark ones in particular).

Dave and Martin would start the challenge in Zermatt but, with Zermatt being exceedingly expensive, we decided to stay in Saas Fee. Even that wasn't cheap. Dave and I would have three days on our own before Martin arrived; however, Dave had instructions to use the time to start an acclimatisation programme. Good preparation would be an important factor in the search of success.

Allalinhorn, at 4027m (13212 ft), is a straightforward mountain if you use the easiest route and therefore perfect for acclimatisation. The men thought that I was capable of climbing this too, so my bystander role started to take on a different form.

Access to the start is via several cable cars and the Metro Alpin, a funicular train which cuts through the mountain taking you to a height of 3445m (11302 ft). This leaves 'only' 600m (1968 ft) on Shanks's Pony. As I stepped off the train, I became light-headed; coming out onto the glacier was breath-taking in more ways than one. It was beautiful but, with approximately thirty-five percent less oxygen compared to sea level, any exercise required far more effort.

By the time I'd put on my crampons and Dave had tied me onto the rope, I was ready for a rest. The scenery was stunning, snowy alpine peaks with clear blue skies, but I couldn't appreciate it as the nerves kicked in.

It would be the first time on a glacier for both of us without the reassurance of Martin's presence. I didn't doubt Dave's ability, but this was a serious playground. There were several crevasses to negotiate, hence the rope; maybe we were being over-cautious but I was happier for it to be that way.

Many people on the mountain didn't care, or were ignorant of, good rope practice; it is easy to become complacent, especially when a place is popular and regarded as an easy route. I didn't rate their chances if they stumbled into a hidden crevasse; mountains have a knack of biting you in the bum when you least expect it.

It was rather like being in a row of ants, plodding along, following the group in front. This is a huge downside to a popular route in a popular area and it's a situation I do not relish; this is where Norway and Scotland come into their own. Occasionally (or frequently, if I'm being honest) we stopped to admire the scenery and to get our breath back. Okay, it was me who stopped to get my breath. Dave seemed absolutely fine, which was so frustrating.

The summit was accessed via a short but very narrow arête (ridge), then it was a case of re-tracing your steps. This meant the arête was busy with people heading in both directions. I had strict instructions from Dave not to be overly polite. The Brits might have many faults but, generally speaking, we queue in an orderly manner. That doesn't apply to all nationalities; several people on the arête had no qualms about pushing past. The fact that there was hardly room for two abreast on the path, with a sheer drop on either side, seemed incidental. I found that so rude but, more to the point, downright dangerous. Dave was my shield and ensured nobody could push in.

It was time to go back down. The nerves had disappeared; I wasn't fighting the altitude and I could appreciate my surroundings – until, *boom*! There was the sound of what seemed to be an explosion.

We stopped dead in our tracks, together with all the other ants on the mountain. Momentarily I wondered if it was the sound of an avalanche. Ahead of us, on a neighbouring mountain, a plume of dust billowed up into the air. Part of the mountainside had sheared off.

Within minutes, bright red helicopters were circling the area. They seemed so small against the backdrop of the landscape. It was uncertain if any climbers had been in the vicinity. We later heard that there were no casualties but it was a sombre reminder to have a healthy respect for the environment.

We spent a considerable amount of time in the various cable cars that take you back into the valley. I'm not a great one for chatting to strangers, I normally leave that to Dave, but exceptions can be made.

'Have you been climbing?' came from behind me.

I turned around to see a drop-dead gorgeous climber who

could have given Ross Poldark a run for his money.

'I see you have an ice screw,' he went on.

Desperately trying to string a coherent sentence together, I managed to explain that my husband had been showing me how to place the screw in the ice. This was partially out of consideration for me but, more importantly, if Dave fell down a crevasse a rescue could involve me using an ice screw. I still wouldn't have rated Dave's chances.

Ross Poldark and I laughed and bantered about other possible uses for an ice screw. Perhaps that's where I'd gone wrong all those years ago before I met Dave: I should have carried an ice screw as an accessory.

Dave was busy talking to the man's wife who, of course, was equally attractive and seemed amused at his broad Yorkshire accent. Finally the cable car deposited us back on terra firma – and back to reality.

Martin was due, as well as our friends Karen and Damien. They'd offered to join us and keep me company as Dave would be tied up for several days with Martin, training for the Matterhorn.

I'd met Karen during my seven years' 'home alone.' We had immediately hit it off on a walking holiday. Although we lived sixty miles apart, that was immaterial to our friendship – and that was in the days when contact was via a landline telephone or a letter in the post. Karen and I have shared many special moments; she is one of the few people who knows nearly all there is to know about me.

The Damien-and-Karen combination was due to a little matchmaking on my part. I could see potential; opposites attract, and it seemed that just a little nudge was required. Their first day out was on a via ferrata (climbing) route in the Lake District, which was admirable considering that Karen is not a lover of heights or climbing. Their mutual interest was walking and ten years later they are still together. This outdoor life has a lot to answer for!

While the three of us had pleasurable and relaxing days, Dave was put through his paces. The Weissmies Traverse managed to rattle even his cage. I have it on good authority that the word 'narrow' didn't do it justice. 'That flippin' ridge' was how Dave described it. (That's not actually the word he used – use your imagination.)

Minutes before they stepped back onto lush green pastures, Dave took a tumble and slammed his elbow onto the ice. This was less than forty-eight hours before he would be climbing the Matterhorn. Dave is stubborn and rarely takes painkillers, but his rules had to be broken. We made a hasty visit to the local pharmacist to purchase an elbow support and, for once, he agreed to take any cocktail of pain relief that I offered him.

A start time of 4.30am in the pitch black is normal for the Matterhorn climb, or rather to join the queue to start the climb. Many climbers stay at the Hörnli hut the night before; however, like many things in Switzerland, the prices are sky high.

Martin planned for the two of them to camp overnight. Unfortunately, where they pitched their tent was a considerable distance away from the start of the climb. There are restrictions on camping any nearer, with hefty fines if you are caught. Although I wasn't climbing, I wanted to be at the base of the Matterhorn to welcome them back. It would also be an enjoyable walk from the Schwarzsee cable car to the Hörnli hut.

On the 16th August, I waved off Dave and Martin from Saas Fee as they headed for Zermatt. I would follow in their footsteps the following day and rendezvous with them by the Hörnli hut in the early afternoon. Damien was happy to accompany me, while Karen opted to stay in Saas Fee.

Damien and I needed to set off quite early. First there was a bus journey of about thirty minutes then an hour's train ride from Stalden-Saas through to Zermatt. Next there was a fifteen-minute walk through Zermatt to the cable-car station and then the cable car up to the Schwarzsee hut. This was where we'd start the two-hour walk before finally arriving at the base of the mountain.

It would have been far simpler to wait for their return to Saas Fee, but it's not every day that your husband climbs the Matterhorn unless you are married to a mountain guide. I also had this picture in my head of us not quite running into one another's arms but something along those lines ... and how romantic to do it by an iconic mountain.

I was so excited as we arrived in Zermatt. It was a glorious sunny day as we marched towards the cable-car station. The chocolate-box image of Switzerland hardly registered; its pristine alpine chalets were adorned with window-boxes full of trailing geraniums. The only thing that marred the scene were the crowds that choked the streets.

My childlike excitement vanished as we caught sight of the Matterhorn. Hell's teeth, it was a magnificent but formidable mountain – and that was from a distance. Even Damien, who can be hard to impress, was taken aback. My excitement changed to horror. To think Dave was up there… Neither of us could take our eyes off it but, horrified or not, we were on a mission.

We bought tickets for the cable car – a bank loan might have come in handy – and we went in search of the victors. The walk from the Schwarzsee hut was well worth the effort; parts looked like a lunar landscape with an array of mountains in the distance, a touch of Norway except for the number of people.

It came as some surprise to find a helicopter 'parked' part way up the mountain. There didn't appear to have been an accident. The mystery was solved as people arrived who seemed to have hired the helicopter as a taxi – more money than sense.

The closer we approached, the Matterhorn took on an even more menacing appearance. It was a pyramid of seemingly impenetrable black rock, with the summit belching out smoke signals or rather a white cloud struggling in vain to escape the mountain's grip.

We arrived at the Hörnli hut where several climbers were sitting around. It was obvious where they had been but they had a variety of expressions on their faces. Sheer joy on some, others apparently traumatised having returned from a living hell.

Damien rummaged in his rucksack to retrieve a pair of binoculars while I rummaged for my lipstick. It might not feature on any kit list, and to be honest it's not on mine, but this was going to be a memorable occasion.

I rarely have my phone switched on when I'm in the mountains but today was an exception. It beeped: a text from Martin. My heart missed a beat and I feared the worst although, in hindsight, you wouldn't text somebody bad news: 'Your husband has just fallen to his death!' To the contrary, the message read: 'Everything okay, running late, too late for the last cable car. Dave and I will camp overnight. Don't wait for us.'

'Put the binoculars away, Damien, they're not coming.' My bottom lip quivered as I tried to explain.

Damien was taken aback but was quick to give me a comforting hug, which was so touching particularly when that isn't his style. Logic isn't my strong point but Damien did his best to reason with me. I had to remember that 'we' were overlooking the obvious: Dave was safe; he had summited; they were well, and it was merely taking longer than anticipated. Surely that didn't matter in the slightest.

Of course Damien was right and talking perfect sense, but it hadn't ended as I had planned. My little bubble had burst and emotions are powerful tools. From disappointment I jumped to my comfort zone of planning. Look hard enough and you will find a solution; there's more than one way to skin a rabbit, etc. How could I meet up with Dave? Got it...

I texted Martin to suggest Damien could return to Saas Fee then I could stay back and camp with him and Dave. Problem solved. The reply was a polite no; it was only a two-man tent and they had few rations. We've had three in a one-man tent and I would share my sandwich, so that was a minor inconvenience in my book.

Poor old Damien was so kind and diplomatic when he said that I had to accept the situation and we both had to return to Saas Fee. I can be quite horrible at times, and I went from tears to renewed hope and then to anger.

'Fine, I shall just trail *all* the way back to Saas Fee after coming *all* this way for nothing. I hope they are comfy in their little tent!' The fact that hundreds have died on that mountain, and both Dave and Martin had been risking life and limb, was forgotten. Oh, and I had overlooked the fact that this challenge wasn't mine. Yes, I needed a slap.

I mellowed as the bus pulled into Saas Fee but, like a dog with a bone, another plan was in the offing. The following morning, I boarded the bus to Stalden-Saas railway station. It was too far to go to Zermatt but I could meet Dave from the train.

Success. First a wave and then a big hug. I stopped short of running down the platform but we did have a kiss more or less under the railway clock, not dissimilar to the one in the old black-and-white film *Brief Encounter*, except our meeting wasn't part of a chaste love affair. I nearly got the fairy-tale ending, and not everyone can say they have been stood up by the Matterhorn! It's funny how things often work out for the best.

Dave was delighted to see me at the railway station but doubted he would have done my original dream scenario justice; it could have ended in tears. He was thrilled at his achievement but physically and mentally shattered once the climb was over; my presence at that moment might not have been fully appreciated. Now he could share his victory with me.

They had met an American on the summit who was keen to know Dave's age. 'I'm sixty-seven,' said Dave. There was a slight pause. With a deflated look on his face, the man revealed he was sixty-four and had hoped to be the oldest person on the summit that day.

It had been by far the most challenging climb Dave had ever done. It sounded horrendous and I was mortified to hear of people attempting to push past them. There had almost been an international incident with climbers going up and also coming down. A near-murderous move was prevented by two simple words: 'Fuck off!' Dave was unsure of the other people's nationality but they got the message. Dave – and I'm fairly sure Martin – rarely swear, but their lives were at stake. Sheer madness.

On the whole, most people climb responsibly; it is only a handful who are total maniacs. Only the week before two climbers had been killed, albeit due to bad weather rather than being selfish morons on the loose. There is a cemetery in Zermatt dedicated to climbers who have lost their lives on the Matterhorn that we visited at a later date. It was so moving. The simplest epitaphs seemed to be the most poignant and brought home the fragility of life. I was a bag of bits by the end. Thank heavens we didn't visit it beforehand.

And just when you think we've finished in the Alps....

In the men's absence, I'd been perusing a guide book on the 4000m-plus peaks in the Alps. The book happened to have been written by Martin. I came across a peak that sounded relatively simple and could be accessed from Saas Fee. I guess you know what's coming: by the time we were back in the village, it was agreed that Martin would guide me up Alphubel the following day. Thinking Dave might be too tired, I was pleasantly surprised when he said he would join us.

The route in mind utilised the Längfluh cable car but unfortunately that was closed for maintenance. No problem: we would use the cable cars and train for Allalinhorn, although this would be a longer route. It also entailed negotiating a narrow ridge, the Feeckopf, before reaching our objective. I'm sure Martin thought he was offering words of reassurance when he likened the ridge to a mini-Cuillin Ridge on the Isle of Skye. Bloody marvellous. That was all I wanted to hear ... but this mountain was my idea, after all. I often play hell about ideas of mine.

It came as a huge surprise when I coped quite well on Feeckopf. The fun didn't start until we were only twenty minutes away from the summit of Alphubel at 4206m (13799 ft). My excuse was that the altitude was getting the better of me – or had I been too ambitious? Just a few steps and I was out of breath. It was a lovely sunny day but I cope far better with the cold. I was so hot and I couldn't have worn any less without scaring my fellow mountaineers.

Martin was very patient and let me stop every few paces. This is the man who climbed all seventy-five 4000m-plus peaks in the Alps in one continuous journey over fifty-four days without the use of a motorised vehicle.

Dave thought he was whispering when he muttered, 'Sue, say if you've had enough. We can go back.' Martin came to an abrupt halt and reminded us firmly that he was in charge and he would decide as and when we turned around! That put Dave in his place. That's why Martin is so good and does his best to get the most out of you. You are so thankful to him ... hours later!

We summited – yippee! Now it was just a matter of retracing our steps. Although we were descending, the many intermediate ups and downs had been erased from my memory. Some of the inclines were negligible, but not according to my lungs or legs.

We were roped up. Dave was leading and I was in the middle. My progress was non-existent; now I know what a puppy feels like when it's being pulled along. All that was missing was the command 'heel'. If Dave pulled once more on my lead, I would kill him if I could get close enough. In his defence, he thought that he was helping by dragging me along. If only somebody would shoot me and put me out of my misery...

We had a serious issue time-wise as we needed to catch the last cable car down, which left at an absurdly early time. We made it with no more than a couple of minutes to spare. The man at the kiosk had closed the barrier but waved us through as he looked quizzically at me; it appeared he hadn't met many people from 'Planet Zog'.

A few hours later, with a glass of red wine in my hand, I commented on what a good day it had been.

007 or 951?

'OH NO,' SCREAMED Lynne, as Carl bawled 'Dave!' Meanwhile I bounced from rock to rock, not knowing what had happened or where I was, though I was making remarkable progress descending head-first down this boulder-strewn gully.

The fall must have lasted only a matter of seconds but that was ample time to deduce that the outcome of this stumble could have serious repercussions. With any luck I would lose consciousness and avoid the excruciating pain that might ensue if I fell any further. Fortunately I felt no pain, despite my anatomy wrestling with the never-ending rocks that adorned this eroded hell-hole.

The absence of pain was uncanny. Many years ago I turned my ankle when only twelve inches off the ground, which resulted in a fracture and my foot at right-angles to my leg. The pain was sickening as I heard the bone crack but that paled into insignificance with the pain I experienced when my foot was straightened without the advantage of intravenous painkillers. That agony was off the scale!

My topsy-turvy world came to a halt. I opened my eyes, realising that I was neither stoking the fires of hell nor chatting with the angels but listening to a mouthful of expletives spewing from Dave's mouth as he stood over me, wedging my body against a boulder. My hero had halted my descent at some considerable risk to himself.

I misinterpreted Dave's rant, convinced he was vexed at my

clumsiness, so my first words were, 'I'm sorry.' Then I realised that there was no annoyance: Dave was shocked. It was tricky to focus as I could not see out of my left eye. It wasn't until Dave took out a hankie and started to wipe my face that I realised it was only blood that was blinding me and nothing more serious.

I tried to move, anxious to escape the gully and the cold trickling water that was cascading over me. I had created a blockage in a tiny mountain stream. Dave was far from happy at the idea I should move, fearing more injury. He was desperate to summon help, something rare for a down-to-earth Yorkshireman. However, after some persuasion verging on insistence from me, it was agreed that I would be manhandled out of the gully before seeking assistance.

It seemed to be a lot of fuss about nothing. I protested that I was okay but sadly nobody else agreed. Lynne, a retired physiotherapist, commented that I couldn't see what I looked like. Charming – and I regarded her as a friend! She also pointed out that nobody knew what was going on inside my head. Dave might easily argue that is a normal state of affairs.

At my third attempt to suggest I could walk a little further, I was told in no uncertain terms that I looked like death warmed up and I was not taking another step. My cunning plan to escape my stone jail and slowly walk back to the car had failed. I had no energy to discuss the matter at length so relinquished the reins and help was summoned. Rescue 951 were on their way.

I was calm but embarrassed; what had I done wrong? How could I be in this situation? Why was everybody over-reacting? As I waited patiently, I recalled the start of what should have been an enjoyable day in the company of friends.

We'd driven into an empty parking area at the side of Loch Slapin on the Isle of Skye. The windscreen wipers, although on maximum speed, struggled to cope with the volume of water falling from the skies. It was September 2016 and Bla Bheinn (Blaven) would be Carl's final Skye Munro. Despite the weather, we had been upbeat about the day ahead and all the mountain weather forecasts had agreed that the rain would pass. We hardy souls left the comfort of the car and faced the elements.

The forecast proved correct. The clouds dispersed, the sky changed from grey to blue and our only concern was how to cross an unavoidable stream. The thunderous noise from the gorge told us that the water was in full spate. Bridges are few and far between in the Scottish Highlands, and today was no exception. Perhaps I am biased about Dave's excellent route-finding skills, but once again he triumphed and the water obstacle was safely negotiated.

We had summited with everyone in good spirits and the bonus of excellent views of the Cuillin Ridge. Admittedly I had my daydreaming head on, having pondered how the Cuillin came under the banner of 'hills'. In my eyes they were, and always will be, mountains: scary, hair-raising ones, yet holding some beckoning, sinister attraction.

We chose Great Gully for our return; perhaps it had been named by somebody with an evil sense of humour? Its appearance was less than pleasing; steep and badly eroded, in hindsight it was better suited to good winter conditions. My daydreaming head had vanished, along with the complacency that Bla Bheinn was easy. The mountains often remind me who is boss and it's certainly not me.

I had followed Dave, with the others behind. A tortoise could have moved faster but they are few and far between, so it didn't matter. A couple of loose rocks overtook us, gaining momentum, but, with much relief, we negotiated the trickiest section. And then...

We heard the sound of an approaching helicopter in the distance. I suggested it might be wise to hold an orange survival bag in the air to help it spot us. I have to say the helicopter was much larger and far more impressive than those in Saas Fee.

Finally my emotions got the better of me as my survival instinct disappeared. I could no longer intervene with the plans. Suddenly I felt very vulnerable and the tears began to fall silently as I started to shake uncontrollably. No amount of a pull-yourself-together attitude worked. Feeling the incredibly strong downdraft from the helicopter, I watched as the winchman was lowered. A couple of our rucksacks were swiftly anchored down before they took flight.

Can fiction become fact? My cloud-cuckoo-land library contains a collection of fantasies, many dating back years. Number 5A features a helicopter. Here we go; I'm looking my bright-eyed and bushy-tailed best, dangling from a winch attached to the likes of Daniel Craig (aka 007) and being whisked away to some exotic destination to be wined and dined. I realise I'd dreamed of this before the knock on the head, but I'm sure that many people have pipe-dreams if only they would admit it.

My winch was not fantasy. A front tooth missing; one eye half-closed as dripping blood blurred my vision; a hole in my head; dried blood gluing my hair to my scalp, and a punctured lip: I was hardly looking my best. Yes, I was whisked away but, kind as they were at Raigmore Hospital, Inverness, I wouldn't categorise that as an exotic destination. Neither was Daniel Craig the winchman; he was called Duncan. However, I certainly would not have exchanged Duncan for 007; he was my knight in shining armour – or rather shining helicopter.

Try as I might, there are still pieces of the jigsaw missing from that eventful day. I vaguely remember the winch. Emotionally, I felt nothing. I could have had a different view of Bla Bheinn if I'd opened my eyes but I didn't, not through fear of swinging in mid-air but of throwing up.

The winch-line started to spin, even though Dave had been given the task of holding a second line which can minimise this problem. Bad enough that I needed help; to vomit would have put the tin lid on it. Having said that, I briefly risked opening my eyes to see the red chevrons on the belly of the helicopter getting ever closer. It seemed I was about to bump my head on the underside of the chopper. It goes without saying that this wasn't the case and I was safely delivered inside.

Dave had been asked to carry back the second line used in the winch that would be dropped off at Portree police station. He was more than happy to help but it was literally a lead weight, and I have it on good authority that it slowed him down. I've often threatened to add bricks to his rucksack in order to reduce his speed; at last it had happened, but I wasn't there to profit from the side effects!

En route to Inverness, Duncan, now wearing his paramedic hat, tended to my injuries. I vividly recall feeling incredibly cold and shaking violently, yet I was numb to the pain I'd felt when I'd staggered out of the gully. In fact, it came as some surprise to discover a very thin layer of skin had been scoured off my lower arm and dried blood had attached my skin to the sleeve of my top.

I shall be eternally grateful for what Rescue 951 did for me. Perhaps the gods were looking down on me that day. I was very lucky to escape the trauma with only stitches, bruising and swelling that a boxer would have been proud of. I was toothless and my pride was well and truly dented, but I had no serious injuries. For once I was grateful not to possess a body resembling a stick insect; some padding came in handy.

We live in a crazy age of health-and-safety madness and I'm the first to criticise the 'wrap in cotton wool' attitude, but my accident made me reflect. It was the only day while we were on Skye that we'd chosen not to wear helmets. I apologised to Duncan for this omission; I felt guilty enough for being in this situation, let alone without a helmet. He smiled and was kind enough not to comment. I felt sure that Martin would be less than pleased after what I'd been taught, but I knew I would have to confess.

I often relive the 29th September. I don't find it upsetting but I doubt that the odd missing pieces of the jigsaw will ever be found. When I see a coastguard rescue helicopter, I mentally give them a wave and wonder whether it's my beloved '007'.

The mountains had given me a gentle kick up the backside. They are still my friends but I need to remember who's boss!

Dave victorious on the summit of the Matterhorn

Martin and Dave safely down near Hornli Hut

Martin and Sue on the summit of Alphubel

Rescue 951 hovering

Start of the winch below Great Gully Bla Bheinn

Mid-air with 007?

Out of Number 5 Gully heading for The Ledge

PART TWO

2017

On the Ledge

Never say Never

These Boots are (not) made for Walking

Mulled Wine and Mince Pies

On the Ledge

I WORRIED ABOUT a possible void in my life after the Munro challenge but I had worried for nothing. 2016 proved to be anything but mundane. Richard, a work colleague and close friend, commented (along with a cautionary note) about striving to live my life 'full of rainbows'.

The excitement and spectacle were undoubtedly an intense thrill but, inevitably, there was a price to pay once they faded away and an emptiness took their place. I confess that he had good reason to make his remark after the times he'd dealt with my mood swings as I went 'cold turkey', desperate for the next fix. I liked to believe that another rainbow would shine before too long.

I suppose my confidence was dented after my accident, although I wasn't aware of the fact. I know I felt guilty for some considerable time, but guilty of what I'm not too sure.

Some wives are treated to a spa day, relaxing and being pampered. Dave had kindly bought me a gift voucher for a day of winter mountaineering with Martin. I certainly wasn't going to be pampered by Martin as we tackled the Ledge route onto Carn Dearg on the north face of Ben Nevis. This would be therapy for my confidence but hardly relaxing!

March 2017, and at 5.45am I was heading to meet Martin near Lochcarron before the drive over to Fort William. It was an unusual situation and a two-edged sword, in that Dave is invariably with me on any of my adventures. This time Dave's comforting presence was absent, but it was replaced with the challenge that I would have to be more self-reliant.

Within minutes of leaving Lochcarron, I had blotted my copy book by eating very little breakfast. Yes, I was aware I needed fuel, but with my nerves jangling and the early departure time, food was the last thing my body craved. However, with a good two-hour drive ahead of us, I promised Martin I would eat along the way.

We made a slight diversion to collect a key to enter a car park that gave better access to the start of the route, a prerogative for mountain guides. The weather was less than perfect: there was a low cloud base and it had started to snow, adding to the considerable amount that had already fallen. It was highly unlikely conditions would improve and the least time bare skin was exposed the better, so, with the advantage of the odd nearby shrub, it was time to head for a pee. No problem except – ah, I was wearing my winter trousers, which require the use of braces. I'll have you know that the Day-Glo green option were a bargain.

There was a technical hitch: I'd forgotten that although I can unclip the braces, Dave normally clips them back on. I've tried before but they twang and disappear up my back, which means taking off my jacket. It was no good: I would have to ask for assistance.

'Martin, I need clipping up.' He obliged. I was missing Dave already!

In mountaineering terms, the Ledge route is at the easy end of the scale; however, I'm sure even seasoned professional mountaineers will tell you that easy routes still require respect. Accidents do happen and can prove fatal. The Ledge route is no exception and, whether it be at the low end of the scale or not, I was apprehensive.

The first half hour was easy, a gentle walk on a path that was some twelve inches underneath the snow. There was too much time for me to ponder on what I was about to do and, with the path not wide enough for two abreast, it was difficult to talk unless I opted for the continental approach and shoved Martin to one side!

There were several people heading towards us as the falling snow intensified, going in the direction of the car park. The conditions did not worry me; I enjoy winter and I had every faith in my leader and his judgement. My disappointment would not, and could not, prevent Martin pulling the plug if safety warranted it.

The meandering on the path was over and now it was time for the serious stuff. We had a quick bite to eat as we prepared for the climb. Helmet (most important!), harness, crampons, ice axe at the ready and attached to a rope. For once I was very efficient in my preparation, which seemed to meet with approval.

Martin pointed out a variety of climbing routes, including where we were heading. Ours looked iffy enough, let alone the more demanding options. Perhaps it was as well that the visibility was poor and the grey clouds partially masked what lay ahead.

Although there was ample snow around us, the inky black buttresses of the north face of 'The Ben' pierced the whiteness, glowering down at us. Not the best of welcoming committees I've encountered. We crossed a burn that was well concealed by the snow and headed in the direction of Number 5 Gully.

Only fifty metres of the gully had to be negotiated before diverting, but that was more than enough. The snow was deep and we were in an area notorious for avalanches. I observed slight movement above us: tiny little snowballs started heading our way, building up momentum, which I calmly pointed out to the boss. I felt sure he was aware of them and my observations were superfluous to requirements, but I would still impart my findings to show I was taking the matter seriously.

'Yes, the sooner we get out of here the better,' came the reply.

A few minutes later we stopped for Martin to put in protection. I'm not the best person to describe this but, for those who are clueless about such things (like me, until recently), I'll do my best. A rope had to be attached to the rock/snow/ice or anything that wouldn't collapse or move so that when Martin negotiated the next section, he would not fall very far if he slipped. This was on the basis that I would be holding part of the self-same rope, feeding out enough of it for him to move but also ready to halt the rope to stop a full fall. This is known as 'belaying' and involves the use of various gizmos: cams, nuts, slings (not triangular bandages) and karabiners, known as krabs to their friends. No wonder climbers don't cover huge distances – they're too busy playing with their gizmos!

The protection was in. Martin went first and I was given instructions to wait for the shout to proceed until he was safe and ready to belay me. Not only that, I also had to remove various bits of this protection. So, Martin was out of sight and there I was 'admiring' my surroundings with a task to carry out that Dave has always taken care of. On paper it was a simple procedure, particularly where I was positioned; I was not hanging off a rock face. But, in the cold light of day it seemed a far more onerous task, especially as I'd developed a nervous shake.

I chattered quietly, telling myself to pull myself together and to get on with it. I knocked out the protection without too much trouble and I had the reassurance of a back-up plan I'd formulated: leave the shackles there and I would buy replacements.

I'd done my best at belaying Martin, threading out rope, etc. He commented cheekily how safe he'd felt with me in charge of the rope. Yeah, I bet… I observed pigs flying past, but it made me smile.

Few words were spoken; I needed to concentrate on every move I made and not waste oxygen on chit-chat. After that section, I thoroughly enjoyed myself and it was steady away to the top. It was time to refuel and, on this occasion, I enjoyed my food. We actually had a lengthy break by Martin's standards; he has an expression I've heard several times: 'This is not a picnic mountain.'

Sadly, the weather wasn't in picnic mode as the snow rapidly turned to rain. Although the summit of Ben Nevis wasn't far away, we decided to give it a miss. In any case, that hadn't been our goal.

There was an option of initially taking the 'tourist path' down, before striking off in the direction of our car; alternatively we could take a more interesting direct route, the North Ridge. I can't recollect if I was given the choice, and I needed to remember that this outing was to boost my confidence, so why choose easy?

It wasn't the best of decisions and, by the end of it, we were both hacked off. I wasn't worried but became more and more annoyed about the terrain beneath my feet: small boulders and scree covered by névé (hard snow) but with a thin layer of soft wet snow on top. Even with crampons on, you still slither and slide. Chunter, chunter, as I trolled down, one minute on my backside, then on my feet, on my backside again and then on my feet.

There was one remaining hurdle to negotiate before the car park: water to cross. We were much further downstream from when we'd crossed the burn earlier in the day, so it would probably be wider and deeper. Although only a few hours had passed since the snow had turned to rain, the volume of water had increased rapidly. It wasn't an unusual situation but it was one to be wary of.

My Munro-bagging days were advantageous again in that I knew what to expect: I was about to get wet. Had we been on the outward journey the boots and trousers might have come off, but the car was in spitting distance. Martin grabbed my arm and we waded through thigh-deep water to the other side.

What another brilliant day!

Never say Never

I CAN BE impulsive but, more often than not, challenges, adventures – call them what you will – have evolved over a period of time. I've lost count of the number of instances where I've been dismissive of activities, only to find myself indulging in them months and often years later.

Old habits die hard. I thoroughly enjoy roughing it in the middle of nowhere, wild camping without facilities, bivvying minus the luxury of a tent, but I would not consider a campsite unless there were no other occupants. I've never been a lover of crowds, perhaps something that was handed down from my childhood. Mum and Dad used to take me and my brother to the coast but away from the popular spots. Hest Bank on the west coast, where there are mudflats and a railway but little else, in preference to Blackpool; Reighton Gap on the east coast rather than Scarborough. The Isle of Wight was a favourite, particularly for Dad with his love of the sea, ships and memories of his days in the Royal Navy as a medic. We enjoyed staying on caravan sites but they were small, out of the way and ones without entertainment.

After my accident on Bla Bheinn, I sent a thank you to Rescue 951. Nothing unusual in that, as I'm quite sure many people would do exactly the same. Little did I know that a simple sentence in the correspondence would plant an acorn for the biggest adventure of my life.

Nepal had been mentioned. For years I'd dismissed the idea

of visiting the Himalaya. I didn't doubt that the scenery was unbelievable and the people second to none for kindness and hospitality, but the thought of paying good money to be more or less guaranteed a dose of Delhi Belly had always dissuaded me.

In my younger days, a few years after Paul's death, I visited Bali with Karen. Most of the time was spent in the bathroom throwing up, and with the squits and my leg in a bucket of ice. I'd been bitten by some tiny beast, which resulted in my leg swelling to twice its size. Even the journey home was a nightmare. We had booked with a little-known but cheap airline, involving a fourteen-hour flight. Half the toilets were out of action, some seats were being de-fumigated for fleas as we boarded, and the inflight entertainment was defunct. The overhead lockers would not close properly, which proved amusing on take-off as belongings cascaded onto unsuspecting passengers below. Please bear in mind this was in the days before I 'did adventure', and I was unaware of the infamous Lukla airport where you take your life in your hands. I vowed Bridlington (or rather 'Brid', as it's fondly known to Yorkshire folk) would get my vote for future holidays.

Karen was a good nursemaid on our travels. I was invariably struck down with some stomach issue despite my best efforts to not drink the water, no ice in drinks, etc. I'm quite sure it had nothing to do with the gin and tonics ... or, as it was in those days, gin and orange.

A refuelling stop was necessary so we had to disembark. My stomach was still a little unstable but the main issue was my leg: it had swollen to such an extent that I could barely walk. I suggested two options to the stewardess: a wheelchair, or let me stay on board. If I was prepared to risk remaining on board during re-fuelling, they would allow it. Fine by me; if the aircraft exploded and I went up in a puff of smoke, at least

I would be out of my misery. Not only that, it would solve another problem.

I was in a relationship at the time with someone I shall call Fred. Just before our flight left the UK, he handed me a marriage proposal in the form of a poem. How much more romantic could you get? A few days later, thousands of miles away and after a meal en route to Bali in a revolving restaurant in Hong Kong, where Karen and I indulged in a few glasses of wine, I sent Fred a message accepting his proposal.

By the time we arrived in Bali, there was a single red rose waiting for me. I should have been over the moon but sadly I was not. I'd fallen in love with the idea of being married again, but I knew Fred wasn't the right one for me. I could blame it on the wine but it was my impulsiveness, desperation, call it what you will, which got me into this pickle.

I had no choice other than tell the truth and break the news to Fred on my return. To make matters worse, he met me at the airport with a bouquet of flowers in his arms. You might hate me now – but please read the book before burning it and please stop sticking pins into my photo!

So, back to the Himalaya. For weeks I was hardly aware of my newly acquired acorn that had set seed although I started to google Himalaya and then visited the Moran Mountain website. If I were to even consider such a place, it would have to be with someone I trusted.

The time came when I needed to run the idea by Dave before I pursued this line of enquiry. Unlike some couples, where there has to be great debate and persuasion before an idea gets off the ground, my concern was the opposite. As expected, there was little hesitation; Dave liked the Himalaya idea.

Could we afford it? Only if our contingency fund was prepared to take a hammering. It depends on what school of thought you belong to: some people wouldn't dream of using their savings for such an unnecessary mission. I sent a rather lengthy email to Martin. Now, when I read it (I kept it as a memento), I realise just how many negative comments and questions I asked. Martin pointed out that I should not feel it was compulsory to visit the Himalaya. That was absolutely correct, but something was telling me that I wanted to do this if I could find a solution to my worries.

My main concern was the Delhi-Belly scenario and possible embarrassment. Also, and to a lesser extent, I was worried about being with strangers who could be far more competent – that would lead to further embarrassment. Bingo! If I was with people I knew, I could cope. The answer was staring me in the face … just book a private trip.

The next question was: did it have to be Nepal? Martin specialises in visiting the Indian Himalaya but not Nepal. The choice was already made; I had made this huge step to get this far so it was immaterial whether it was Nepal or India.

I couldn't wait to put the idea to the friends I had in mind to accompany me. Carl's reply was along the lines that he was busy bagging Munros but why not? Put his name down. Anita was surprised but, after some consideration, said yes. Lynne was stunned and wondered if she'd heard correctly; 'Sue, you've always said you would NEVER go there.' But yes, she would definitely be up for it.

Lynne is a comparatively new friend and yet it feels like we have always known each other. It goes without saying that we met when out on the hills. Lynne is a natural climber but often doubts her abilities. Her love of adventure, even as a child, is my total opposite but we gel. One common factor is that we are both habitual worriers; as one concern is solved, we will find something else to fret about. Oh, and Lynne is also now on the Munro-bagging trail!

So, taking Martin into the equation, there would be three

women and three men. Not that the ratio should have a bearing on the success of the trip. Dave and I are lucky in having like-minded interests, or at least that makes for an easier carry-on when we're booking a trip. Both Anita and Lynne were fortunate as their husbands were more than happy to have peace and quiet, home alone either playing golf or watching sport whilst their wives slogged up some mountain in a foreign land. Carl was free as a bird, divorced, and theoretically could do just as he liked, although Anita and Lynne would keep him in check. I would occasionally help out with advice; after all he'd be lost without female guidance and, deep down, I'm sure he enjoyed the attention!

Martin had mooted the possibility of visiting the area of Sikkim, a place he'd never been and where few people go. All this would be investigated at a later stage. A booking was made on the basis that we weren't too concerned where in India we went but the expedition should involve trekking and a peak we could attempt to climb. The peak was the one stipulation Dave and I had, while Anita and Lynne were keen on trekking to be included. Carl seemed happy whatever. Only fifteen months until the big adventure – and the first time I would truly use the word 'expedition' without exaggeration.

These Boots are (not) made for Walking

WE DIDN'T EXPECT to receive further details of our trip for some time. It was now June 2017 and we weren't leaving for India until late September the following year. However, Martin was prompt in supplying a kit list which proved to be an extremely sensible strategy. Although we possessed most of the gear he'd listed, there were a few items we needed to buy. They all related to cold conditions; to have the widest possible choice, we needed to purchase them when the shops were focused on the forthcoming winter season. Little did I know that boots could become such a talking point and the basis of nightmares…

There are many categories of boots, from those suitable for an amble on well-made paths on low-level routes to boots worn on K2 and Everest. We owned both B1 and B2 boots. Our kit list stated B3 and they had to be suitable for altitudes over 5000m (16404 ft). This equated to the insulation in the boot; I discovered there are B3 boots on the market without sufficient insulation, then there are boots that jump into another category with too much insulation. Well, I say too much; it means the prices jump to £700 and more. That would have been an easier pill to swallow if they were to be worn frequently, but this wasn't so in my case. This would be a one-off expedition.

There appears to be a gap in the market from boots suitable up to 5000m (16,404 ft) and those suitable for over 7000m (22965 ft.) After much research, I found a handful that matched the criteria – only to find they were not available in smaller sizes.

Sod's law, eh? My feet are small and for once I wished I took a larger size. I wish the same could be said about my other bits!

Those offered in smaller sizes were a slim fit. My feet aren't wide but they're not slim either. This search was fast becoming a serious affair. There was an option to hire boots but the websites I looked at didn't appear to have what I needed, and hiring charges weren't cheap. To ensure comfort and fit would necessitate hiring them for a test drive prior to the expedition. Poor Lynne found herself in the same predicament; she gained from having slim feet but took an even smaller size.

At last, with the help of a wonderful independent shop in Keswick, I found some boots. Heavy and substantial, but they fitted; my feet were comfortable and the boots were a snip at £350. Dave had even more luck and found a pair that weighed less than mine, but beggars can't be choosers and at least I'd been shod. Anita faired rather better since her larger feet gave her a better choice. Her husband had palpitations when he espied well over a £1000 pounds worth of new boots lined up in the hallway. 'You can't keep them all, Anita!'

It was early December and, with the first fall of snow, an ideal opportunity to try out the B3s. In this day and age, most boots require no breaking-in but I felt these might be an exception. Ullock Pike and onto Skiddaw in the Lake District would do nicely. Crampons would also be required so it was an ideal practice trek, and just how it would be in the Himalaya, excluding altitude and crevasses.

The start of the walk was scuppered by a road closure but the only consequence was a revised starting point that added another mile. As we'd hoped, there was plenty of hard snow and ice underfoot. The crampons went on; it was lovely to feel secure and stable as people slithered by with no crampons and wearing glorified trainers. Fortunately, they had the sense to turn back. In fact, one gentleman commented on our footwear:

'What are those metal things on your feet? I need some of those.'

I was upbeat about the day; we were more than well-equipped and it was the start of our preparation for the Himalaya. The only slight niggle was just how much effort lifting my feet required. The boots and the crampons together weighed a considerable amount but at least my feet were comfortable. No matter; we weren't in a rush and it was a beautiful day.

To hell with 'beautiful day'! By the time we reached the summit of Skiddaw, I was in agony. My feet were okay but the tendons leading from my outer ankle felt as though a knife had been inserted in them. So much for my earlier smugness; now the thought of glorified trainers seemed very appealing even if they were potentially lethal.

It seemed an eternity as I hobbled back; progress was painfully slow and the day, which had now changed into a starlit night, did little to ease the torment. Trying different combinations of lacing techniques was futile, Dave suggested a variety of possibilities, only to be met with an ungrateful retort of 'Don't be ridiculous, that won't work!'

Stopping to put on our headtorches was a good excuse to rest. The thought of going barefoot crossed my mind, particularly when I remembered there was also the delight of an additional mile to walk.

It is rare for Dave to drive if I'm there; I enjoy driving so he leaves it to me. Not on this occasion. Off with the bastard boots and my legs would not be moving one inch. Nancy Sinatra's boots might have been made for walking but she was obviously not wearing B3s.

Much as I would have loved to set fire to the boots, the problem would have to be resolved. If at first you don't succeed... I decided that my ankle and lower leg needed protection in the form of cushioning. Not enough and it wouldn't work, but too much could exacerbate the situation. Ankle supports could be ideal.

With renewed hope, and now the proud owner of these items, a second attempt was made to master the boots. This time Whernside in the Yorkshire Dales would be the test track and I would go prepared with a spare pair of comfortable boots. More weight, but a small price to pay for some reassurance.

My heart sank as the shooting pain returned when we reached the summit. Why did it happen at the furthest point away from the start? With much relief, in more ways than one, I changed into my 'slippers'. The supports had helped but the pain had moved further up my leg.

I now possessed a variety of supports and socks which all helped to some extent but not sufficiently so. The final straw was the third practice on Pen-y-Ghent, the one you may recall all those pages ago.

This had become a war between me and the boots – and I wasn't prepared to surrender. Drastic measures were needed. 'Dave, I need a sharp knife.' Poor Dave was unsure of my intentions. Was it my leg or my boots that were about to meet their maker?

I deduced that the cuff of the boot came too high up my leg. Cut the thing off; I couldn't change my anatomy so the boots would have to change. Realising only the boots were in for the chop, Dave dissuaded me from doing a DIY job. I was in need of a good old-fashioned cobbler, not just somebody who uses stick-on soles and charges a fortune but a craftsman.

A little internet surfing and I found somebody in Barnard Castle, a town seventy miles away from us. Perhaps I was losing the plot but this was a desperate situation. It was the first time the cobbler had been asked for an alteration of this nature but a week later, and at the very reasonable cost of £25 (excluding petrol), the boots had been transformed. Not everyone owns a pair of B2¾ boots and the trimming helped reduce the weight. As for the £70 spent on supports and socks,

I've written that off to experience. Before you lose the will to live, I can assure you the matter of the boots is now closed!

On the Ledge Route

Looking down Deep South Gully, Beinn Alligin

Sue and Lynne at the top of Deep South Gully

View of summit of Sgùrr a'Ghreadaidh - the Cuillin Ridge, Isle of Skye.
(Shame about my 'Blancmange Syndrome'!)

View from our bivvy site on Beinn Tarsuinn

Sunset seen from Beinn Tarsuinn summit

View from A' Mhaighdean - Fisherfield Six

Heavenly lochans espied after leaving Ruadh Stac Mor summit

Mulled Wine and Mince Pies

AFTER THE FOOTWEAR fiasco, Dave and I were looking forward to spending Christmas in Scotland. We had always spent the festive season at home but 2017 seemed to be the year for abandoning convention and we were heading for a favourite cottage in Kingussie that we used regularly in our Munro-bagging days. Carl was joining us; with no family ties, it would be an ideal opportunity for him to tick off a few more mountains.

My daydreaming head was back on as I pictured us perched on top of a snowy-white mountain on Christmas Day with not a soul in sight. However, if Christmas Eve was anything to go by, things weren't looking too promising. It was raining so much that the route we'd planned for Carl to bag a Munro had to be revised. With a burn to cross and water wherever you looked, it would be out of the question.

'Plan Z' came into play and I'm proud to say that it was me who came up with the new version. The days when I never questioned a route had long since disappeared. There were no streams to cross, though it would add a good hour on to the day. The third option of staying in the cottage, nice as it was, certainly wasn't on the menu.

The thought of my picture-postcard Christmas Day was looking very doubtful. However, dreams can come true; as we headed to Glen Feshie the following morning in search of Sgòr Gaoith, the mountains were white and it was snowing.

I suggested we took the less-direct but scenic route, which the men agreed to. For those who know that area, we went via Geal Charn, Meall Buidhe, and we planned to serve Christmas dinner on Sgoran Dubh Mor. I remembered from previous visits that there were plenty of rocks that would do nicely as a table and, in practical terms, could offer some protection from the elements. After our meal, it would be onto Sgòr Gaoith.

The mist was down but that gave more atmosphere to the day. The rocks were sporting their own Christmas decorations, with frost and ice forming charming sculptures. There was snow wherever you looked, and we had the whole place to ourselves.

Just because we were outdoors did not mean standards had to slip and we weren't lacking in seasonal treats: a flask of mulled wine; Christmas crackers with matching serviettes; mince pies and sausage rolls; Christmas cake and cheese (Yorkshire folk eat fruitcake with cheese); cocktail sausages; chocolates; a present each and a hipflask containing whisky. Oh, and I nearly forgot, battery-operated fairy lights. No wonder the rucksacks were heavy. I confess that, when I was divvying out the supplies back at the cottage, I gave myself the serviettes and Christmas crackers to carry; the men were given the mulled wine and heavier items.

Our festive buffet over and it was back to the Munro-bagging business for Carl. Every so often the mist lifted to reveal snow cornices (shelves of snow protruding from solid ground, to be avoided at all costs!) suspended from the crags looking down onto Loch Einich. Then the curtains closed as quickly as they opened, and it was back to little visibility as we headed to Sgòr Gaoith.

Well, blow me down! A solitary figure appeared from out of the mist, heading in our direction. Merry Christmas greetings were exchanged; apparently he'd heard us enjoying our little party but couldn't see us. I'm afraid he'd missed out on the mulled wine but he might be in a luck if he fancied a mince pie. A quick rummage in the rucksack and, lo and behold, I produced a slightly battered mince pie that was more or less in one piece. He seemed pleased – and then speechless when I had another rummage and handed him a Christmas cracker. His only requests were that I pulled the cracker with him and somebody took a photo of the occasion because his friends wouldn't believe him without the evidence. If only everybody was so easily pleased.

I am fully aware I could have worded the cracker affair quite differently, but I shall rise above such temptation! I managed to drop a less-than-subtle hint that I had written a book about bagging the Munros. I wonder if he ever bought a copy of *Head for the Cloud*? Enough of the blatant advert.

It was slightly less romantic on the return leg. Darkness had fallen and the snow turned to rain as we lost height; on a badly eroded path, that meant mud. However, Christmas hadn't totally vanished because it can be magical walking with just a headtorch to light your way. Plus I'd taken the snowflake-shaped fairy-lights and this seemed the perfect moment to use them, so they were strung around my rucksack. Even the men thought they were rather pretty. Either that, or they dared not say anything to the contrary. We'd been out for many hours but that was the best Christmas Day I can remember.

PART THREE

2018

False Start

Geared Up

Fit to Drop

Strength through Misery

Hot in the Highlands

Beware The Ides of Number 29

We Shall Overcome

False Start

TIME HAD SLIPPED by since booking the Himalaya trip. Now we were in 2018, with only months until the big adventure. Before I could concentrate all my efforts on India, however, we were spending three days with Martin in Scotland. This had been booked before the Himalaya trip had even been thought about. In the light of how I performed over those three days, I'm not sure Martin would have been so keen to take me abroad.

The first day went fairly well, at least I thought it did. I am a slow, nervous starter but once I got into the swing of Deep South Gully, which tops out between two of the Horns of Alligin, I was enjoying myself.

Mini-avalanches cascaded down and at one point Martin jumped aside to avoid the debris, at the same time instructing us to stay protected by some rocks. It all added to the excitement. Admittedly there was less enthusiasm once we were at the top of the gully when he pointed out our line of descent. I looked in disbelief; surely we were not going down there! It appeared far too steep for a descent.

Martin piped up, 'Come on, chop chop, we haven't got all day.' If I rushed this, I would be going down head first and faster than I cared to. Been there, got the T-shirt – although this time I was attached to a rope and had my helmet on. We negotiated the descent at a pace we felt happy with, and were instructed only once more to be a little quicker.

Martin asked what we had in mind for the following day. I

suggested popping over to the Isle of Skye and helping Lynne with her Munro bagging. How about Sgùrr a'Ghreadaidh and his sidekick Sgùrr a'Mhadaidh on the Cuillin Ridge? I still have no idea why I said that. After climbing them in good summer conditions when Dave and I were on the Munro trail, I'd vowed I would not be returning, certainly as far as Sgùrr a'Ghreadaidh was concerned. Now I'd just suggested this route in full winter conditions. I'm sure I have a screw loose at times.

The conditions were perfect and I was upbeat. Even the gully we climbed was more than acceptable, except for trying to get out over a cornice. I think Martin fell soft for just a few seconds when he helped me drag myself over the shelf.

Unfortunately, my confidence took a downward spiral as we reached the apex of the arête. I remembered from my first visit that it was narrow, but without snow it was possible to walk slightly to the side. Exposure doesn't bother me, providing I have a firm footing; teetering and balancing directly on top of anything and I get a wobble on. Using trekking poles lessens the blancmange syndrome.

With the arête plastered in snow, the only choice was to go on top of it. I was roped up and had my ice axe out, but without trekking poles (it's bad form to use them in such places) and wearing crampons, I felt unsteady to the extent that I was fighting back the tears. Would somebody please get me off here? What a crazy idea of mine!

I was dreading retracing my steps as that meant going down the arête, which is far more off-putting than going up it. I'm not sure whether a slug is slower than a snail but both of them would have beaten me going down. My skeleton would still be there but for the fact that Martin persuaded me we needed to make some progress. I say you can't rush these things!

Once off the arête, I was fine. There was sufficient wobble room and I could wobble to my heart's content.

It was the final day and mentally I was going downhill. Initially I enjoyed practising crevasse rescue and the principles behind it. This was possible with no crevasses readily to hand by improvised use of the land and using our imagination. A bit of abseiling was next on the agenda using a snow bollard. That in itself was not an issue; the problem was that once I was at the bottom of the cliff face, I would need to climb back up it. It looked a long way down and was nearly vertical, but then most things look vertical to me.

That was it; by the time the various ropes and protection had been sorted out, I'd had too much time to think. Why go down knowing I'd be busting a gut to climb back to where I had happily been standing only minutes earlier? I went on strike; I was not going down there. My body language said it all and Martin accepted my decision.

It was not my best performance. At the end of the three days, when Martin chatted about the Himalaya trip, he gently reminded me that a positive outlook would be vital in India. It was an uncomfortable wake-up call but I promised myself, and Martin, that is exactly what I would do – be positive.

Geared Up

THERE HAD BEEN several emails regarding our proposed destination and what might be possible – it could be some time before Martin actually knew himself. The area of North Sikkim had been mentioned. Everything hinged on the political and military stability of the area and, at the start of the year, Sikkim was looking highly unlikely due to unrest.

In the following months, Martin liaised with his man in India, a gentleman by the name of Mr Pandey. Many trips to the Himalaya take a minimum of three weeks because of practicalities regarding distances and the necessity to acclimatise. Our trip had to be over eighteen days, which gave Martin another obstacle to overcome.

Carl, the youngest of our group at the age of sixty, was the only one who was still in full-time employment and he would struggle to be granted more leave. I still worked three days a week on the admin side for a large corporate law firm but my employers were more understanding. The remaining three were retired.

The boots had been sorted but we required other items of gear. Again, these related to cold weather and we hoped the winter sales would throw up a few bargains. I'm not a lover of shopping at the best of times, and the thought of the sales fills me with dread, but this year would be an exception. We had a list of requirements and spent hours researching what was on offer. As and when something took somebody's eye, a message was sent to the team. The WhatsApp group was unimaginatively called 'Expedition' (I spent all of five minutes thinking of a title) with a photo of Everest as its logo. As far as we were concerned this was going to be our Everest and regardless of where we ended up, the shopping list remained the same.

The shopping system worked well but for the fact that our kit was rather like a school uniform: same gloves, same sleeping bags, same down jackets. Even the equipment we already owned was often the same. Very early in the proceedings, it became apparent that items would have to be tagged for identification. The military manage it, so why couldn't we? Our efficiency might not be quite as slick but we'd give it our best shot.

We knew we'd have the advantage of porters (and high-altitude porters) who would carry the communal gear such as tents, food, ropes, cooking equipment, and help transport the items that we didn't need on a daily basis. We would be responsible for carrying most of our own personal kit. The weight we were expected to carry was a particular concern to Anita and Lynne, although Martin assured us we'd be looking at no more than about twelve kilos each and it would be on a sliding scale. Petite Lynne could hardly carry the same as Dave and Carl. In the early days there had been talk of the need for 60–80 litre rucksacks. I think Lynne would fit inside one that size!

It's hard to imagine how difficult it can be to find a rucksack that suits your needs. Go into any outdoor shop and you seem to be spoilt for choice – unless you are called Lynne. Half the battle of finding a comfortable rucksack is how it fits your back. Diminutive Lynne, at four feet eleven inches, has always had problems finding one that is short enough in the back. They are few and far between, even for 35–40 litre bags; start to look at 50–60-plus litre rucksacks and it's mission impossible. Lynne scoured shops and websites for over six months; her rucksack had to fit but also needed to be as light as possible before it was filled with the gear.

Anita, being a good five feet eight inches, had no problems with back length but, like Lynne, is very slim in build with little padding and had issues with the weight of a load. For once I was at an advantage. At nearly five feet two, I was okay when it came to back length and my built-in padding benefited me when carrying loads. My extra ballast has often been helpful when we're out in cold, windy conditions because I can withstand the gusts and I'm well insulated.

When it comes to most equipment, better quality and the least possible weight equate to serious money. We all budgeted for the trip but, in a very short space of time, the budget went out of the window. I bought an Exped Thunder 70-litre sack, not cheap but it fitted well and was light in weight. Carl bought the same. Lynne finally chose the 50-litre version, which shortened sufficiently to fit her tiny frame. Anita used a 58-litre sack and Dave had a 60-litre. How come mine was larger than Dave's? Although I like 'rummage room', mine was still lighter.

One item that wasn't on the kit list, but was one of the first items I bought, was a flag. I would have been quite happy to take the Union Jack but I wanted this to be rather more personal, so it would be the Yorkshire flag, the White Rose. I would risk Martin's wrath at carrying unnecessary items. I had no idea which peak we would summit but, whichever it was, I would be there flying my flag.

The next item on the shopping list was a headtorch. Dave was quick to point out that the one I already had, which was the same as his, was more than adequate so why buy another? But I'd been dazzled in more ways than one by Anita's headtorch; she was delighted with its performance and used it many times.

Mine was good but, in comparison, it paled into insignificance. In the great scheme of things, to hell with the expense; I would buy one. Lynne followed suit and, with three identical headtorches, we would light up the night sky.

Fit to Drop

BEFORE THE ITINERARY got a look-in, we had to disclose various medical conditions to Martin and our travel insurers: Anita and Carl with their asthma; Lynne with a blood disorder, and I'd recently been told I had raised blood pressure although it didn't require medication. Dave didn't seem to have any problems except selective hearing when I was about! I hate age to become an excuse for anything, but the fact the youngest of us was sixty and Dave the oldest at sixty-nine had to be a consideration. Martin happened to be in the same age bracket – I don't want you thinking we were going with a youngster!

It was time to start thinking about injections. We had a list of those that were essential and those that were optional. Anita and Lynne's main concerns about the trip might have been related to weighty rucksacks and how cold it could be, but mine was health. If there was any injection, pill or potion that could prevent illness, put my name down for it. Essential or optional, Dave and I were going for the whole shebang.

I also discovered something called Bimuno Travelaid, which could reduce the risk of stomach issues. I'd have some of that, too. When it came to the vaccinations, several entailed two or three doses with specific time lapses between. My diary had never seen so many entries but that was the only way I could keep track. Fortunately needles don't worry me; in fact, I like to observe the different techniques. By the time we finished, the bank balance was looking pretty sickly, though, and we were a good £700 worse off. I thought I would be indestructible after this lot – and the budget had well and truly been abandoned.

So, we had a kit list, information about health and a general idea of our itinerary. There was also mention of training for the expedition: running, cycling, attending a gym, in addition to all-round hill fitness. I sent a copy to Diane, a friend I'd known since I was sixteen and met when I worked for Barclays. Rest assured, Diane and her husband Glynn know everything about me, the good, the bad and the ugly, but bless them, they are still there. Diane met Glynn when we were on holiday in Gibraltar in 1974. Glynn was in the Royal Navy and his ship had docked in Gib. (I wonder if The Buccaneer pub is still there?)

The phone rang. 'Susan,' Diane has always used my full name, 'which of these activities are you concentrating on?' She fought back laughter. She knew very well I wasn't a runner, that I'd never learned to ride a bike, had never set foot in a gym and had no intention of changing.

Glynn found it hard to believe I was going to India and joked he would love to be a fly on the wall to observe how I would perform in such basic conditions. It was one thing spending a couple of nights in the wilds of Scotland; the Himalaya, experiencing its simple lifestyle, would be a whole new ball game.

For a while I ignored the subject of training but I knew that I would need to address the problem sooner rather than later. The only way would be with a logical mind. Running really did not appeal, and there was a risk of injury as I was totally new to the game. It was also late in the day to start learning to ride a bike. When it came to gyms, my fear was being surrounded by Lycra-clad athletes half my age and that I wouldn't push myself hard enough if I was left to my own devices.

I was overlooking something: this was a challenge and it was time to venture out of my comfort zone. Forget the running; an exercise bike might do the trick. After making some enquiries, I found that a neighbour had one I could borrow. The electronics didn't work so there was no information about pulse rate, mileage or anything else, but the pedals still functioned. I think it was beneficial not knowing the details.

After some investigation, I found a gym ten miles away that I liked the look of; it appeared down to earth and, after visiting it, I was delighted to see normal people there with less-than-perfect physiques. There was no Lycra in sight and I was by no means the oldest.

I booked in with a personal trainer, something I never thought I'd do, but if the gym was going to do me any good I needed someone to force me into a regime. His name was Matt and it turned out he'd played rugby for South Africa. Perhaps this fitness lark wasn't so bad after all – although I suspect I would have thought differently had my trainer been fit and female!

Strength through misery, as our good friend Damien would say. That certainly applies to exercise bikes and training sessions. I thought I was fairly fit but just sitting on the saddle was agony and that was before pushing the pedals. As for Matt, he was a charming man with a lovely glint in his eye; the term 'smiling assassin' sums him up nicely. As I quickly found out, he didn't miss a trick when it came to cheating or trying to take shortcuts. Why cheat when the only person who'd suffer in the long run would be me? Although occasionally, a few seconds of light relief were very tempting! Funnily enough, a similar comment was mentioned in the Munro-bagging days. How does anybody know you have climbed them? Quite true, but if you lied you'd only be cheating yourself.

Our enjoyment of being on the hills and mountains was still high on the agenda but outings had a slightly different slant because they were part of the training schedule. Nearby Pen-y-Ghent was perfect for a regular half-day sprint for Dave and

I but, on one of our many visits, I was reminded of the fact it wasn't for pleasure.

We weren't wearing the dreaded boots and had left the winter gear behind as we concentrated on speed. I envied the people we passed who were taking their time, admiring the scenery, stopping if they fancied a natter. Make way: we were on a mission with our bright-red faces, tongues hanging out and dripping with sweat. We dreamed that one day we too would stroll up Pen-y-Ghent without looking at our watches.

I dispensed with using trekking poles, which I had come to rely on rather too much over the years. They were intended to take the pressure off the knee joints on steep descents and, to a lesser degree on ascents, but as time elapsed I'd started to use them all the time. My balance was terrible without them and my legs were considerably weaker. For the first few outings my legs felt the strain.

The fitness regime was all-encompassing. As time went by, the group had a slightly different outlook on what should or shouldn't be done, particularly when it drew closer to the expedition. Some relished big days out and pushing themselves to the limit, while Dave and I became paranoid about possible injury. The thought of missing the trip didn't bear thinking about. Crazy, really: we could just as easily fall in the street or even on Pen-y-Ghent, but we decided on little and often and very little scrambling of any nature.

There was another aspect to our training. Martin had strongly recommended we would benefit from altering our diet to include lentils, beans, curry and spices and reduce our intake of meat. This could improve our chances of adapting more easily to the food we would be eating. I would do exactly as I was told about anything that would help me avoid stomach issues – which would make a change!

Before I bore you any further with details of equipment,

shopping, health and fitness, it's time to deviate slightly to a couple of more interesting subjects. Wellbeing comes into the equation but it doesn't take the leading role…

Strength through Misery

SCOTTISH TRIPS WERE still on the agenda. Carl and Lynne were on the Munro-bagging trail and we didn't require a reason to head north. I could not imagine life without visits to Scotland. It would be good training and early May was not too near our departure date.

Eight of us headed to the north-west including Karen and Damien, who you've already met, and Lynne's husband, Phil. He's a man of few words, tells it as it is, but I've never heard him complain though I'm sure Lynne might tell a different tale. Phil is not a lover of bad weather and the thought of snow and ice sends shivers down his spine; however, he is always more than happy to join us out of the winter season. The month of May might be spring south of the border but I told Phil that we could encounter snow. My conscience was clear; he had been warned.

I'd found a lovely property near Gairloch: six bedrooms, five bathrooms and overlooking the sea, ideal for anybody wanting to have a leisurely day. Perhaps Phil might make good use of this option – but that didn't happen; it was his dear wife Lynne who benefited.

Lynne had returned from a walking trip in Spain where she'd stumbled on a low-level path, resulting in tears in her ankle ligaments and two large calf muscles. She could hardly put one foot in front of the other, let alone climb a mountain. Her 'to do' list for Munro bagging had vanished. There was no point in her staying at home to read books or the like; she could be beside the sea and have the pleasure of our scintillating company. It was very much a case of 'salt in the wound' when Phil headed for the mountains and Lynne couldn't, especially as Phil had no interest in the bagging lark. There was some small comfort in that she had nearly five months for her injury to heal before the expedition.

On a couple of 'bagging days', we had less than ideal conditions when Phil experienced the delights of the white stuff. It was the horrible, soft, wet variety; he was not best pleased and told Lynne quite categorically that he would not be doing a re-run. She would be on her own when she came to bagging them.

To be honest, Phil fared well on one particular day. He never objected, although I'm not too sure what was going through his head. I think, unless you were Munro bagging or had masochist tendencies, you would have every right to be hacked off at the end of what turned out to be a mini-expedition...

The combination of Cona' Mheall and Am Faochagach is not a partnership made in heaven but, because of Carl's long-term strategy of Munros (the one he was keeping for last and those he had already done), we faced this unlikely twosome.

Seven of us set off a few hundred yards north of Torrandhu bridge on the A835. It wasn't easy underfoot through bog and heather and traversing the side of the loch. After a couple of hours, Karen had a change of heart. Damien being a true gent (yes!) accompanied her back. Then there were five.

We reached the ridge we were aiming for at a jaunty angle, not quite as we would have liked. There were intimate encounters with heather up the nostrils for longer than I would have wished but, after much huffing and puffing, I was on solid ground.

Good old Scotland; just when you think you have cracked it,

another hurdle appears. The cloud descended, the temperature dropped and this easy rocky ridge developed a sheen of ice. The last time I'd been there was on a lovely sunny day when the rock was dry and it was a joy to troll along. 'Jekyll and Hyde' is an appropriate analogy for life in the mountains; I have been privileged to experience many pleasurable times but also, in contrast, some intimidating and dangerous moments.

It was snowing on the summit of Cona' Mheall. Visibility was non-existent but we needed a break. On more than a couple of occasions we'd agreed to press on just a little further and then a bit further still, never quite finding the ideal spot, but that tactic is not always the best. Lethargy, thirst and hunger can lead to mistakes. In this instance, however, the glass was half full – and it was a golden opportunity to test drive my new emergency survival shelter. Why I hadn't bought one sooner I have no idea; it weighs little more than a bivvy bag but is so much easier to use.

While I was enjoying my sarnies, snug in my little house, Dave went to suss out our escape off dear Cona' Mheall. I'd already come up with a much easier option, albeit not ideal: the second Munro would be aborted and it would entail thumbing a lift back to our car. Dave's route would take us where we needed to be.

Crampons on, ice axes out, and Phil had a crash course in winter skills, including stepping backwards down a snowbank. He did brilliantly and, under Dave's supervision, wasn't fazed in the slightest. Whether he would ever speak to me again was another matter.

That was the only snow we came across. Within an hour the sun appeared, coats were off and we were treated to picturesque views looking down on Loch Prille. From a distance it was difficult to work out how we could cross the loch as it ended abruptly at a waterfall that dropped a considerable way. Anita and I were more concerned than the men until a few stepping stones poked their heads out of the water. We chose to ignore the fact they were perilously close to the head of the waterfall. I'm pretty sure this crossing would be impassable if the water was high – it's another fond reminder of what Munro-bagging can entail.

Having already lost the will to live at times, I knew we still had one last hurdle to negotiate: a stream/river with a reputation for being difficult to cross and, of course, no bridge. Fortunately water levels were low and we were armed with sandals. Sod the sandals: this was another thigh-deep crossing and, fitness regime or not, I used the trekking poles. We squelched back to the car just before night descended, nearly thirteen hours after we left it. Phil's only words were, 'I'm not going anywhere tomorrow.'

We shared cars that day. Damien hadn't taken his and we'd forgotten to give him and Karen the key to our car when they left us. They'd hitched a lift as far as the pub in Dundonnell, fifteen miles down the road, and whiled away a few hours eating, drinking and waiting for us. I don't think they were overly enamoured of our late arrival but it would have been worse had there not been a pub. Gairloch, where we were staying, was another thirty-five miles further on. It's a funny breed of folk who revel in the Scottish mountains.

Hot in the Highlands

JULY 2018. GOING for an enjoyable day out on the hills was now a distant memory. Where we went was immaterial; distance, speed and/or carrying a heavy load took precedence. Nevertheless, a plan was in the offing which ticked all the boxes, including pleasure, and there would not be a gym or an exercise bike for miles.

The weather was looking good and Dave and I fancied some wild camping and bivvying in the north-west highlands that included 'The Fisherfield Six' route. It consists of six mountains, five of which hold Munro status, and was therefore an ideal opportunity for Lynne to bag a few more. Her injuries were well on the way to recovery; when asked if she fancied joining us on a trip north, she replied before I finished my sentence!

The Fisherfield Six can be completed within a day by the very fit. That was us out of the equation, but where there's a will there's a way. Once more the thinking cap came out of the cupboard.

Day One: Drive 390 miles from Yorkshire to Corrie Hallie, walk into Abhainn Loch an Nid and camp.

Day Two: First four mountains – Beinn a'Chlaidheimh, Sgùrr Ban, Mullach Coire Mhic Fhearchair. Bivvy overnight on Beinn Tarsuinn.

Day Three: Remaining two mountains – A'Mhaighdean, Ruadh Stac Mor. Walk back to the tent and stay overnight.

Day Four: Walk back to Corrie Hallie and drive home to Yorkshire.

Surely the stamina and endurance required for this foray would meet the Himalaya training criteria. Our speed might not make the Moran grade, but you can't win them all.

I won't expand on the ins and outs of the route but it was the one and only visit to Scotland when we struggled to find water. Small burns were non-existent and rivers were streams. Even the bogs had dried up. After the third mountain, Mullach Coire Mhic Fhearchair on day two, we were forced to make a detour to a promising watering hole. The water was shallow and teeming with tadpoles but needs must. After more or less sieving the water to extract our little friends, Dave made a brew before we headed to Beinn Tarsuinn, our last stop of the day and where we bedded down for the night. The conditions could not have been better and it was the first time Lynne had bivvied; what an idyllic place, especially for your first time.

The following morning we left Tarsuinn with very fond memories. Sadly, by the time we staggered to the summit of A'Mhaighdean with the sun beating down and still little to drink, my enthusiasm for the Fisherfield Six was waning rapidly. The awe-inspiring views of the Great Wilderness and having the place to ourselves saved the day but did little to quench my thirst.

Ruadh Stac Mor would be number six. Yet again potential water supplies had vanished until a heavenly sight came when we reached the summit: to the north-east, two lochans (small lakes) were shimmering in the sunshine. Admittedly they were some way below but in the direction that we needed to go.

The distance and descent required to get to the damn things were extremely misleading. Dave was way ahead of Lynne and me. Chunter, chunter, as I negotiated boulder after boulder – and still the lochans seemed just out of reach; was I witnessing a mirage? I needed water sooner rather than later.

We lost sufficient height; now there was the small matter of locating a breeze to keep the midges and horseflies at bay. You can't beat winter: plenty to drink, little overheating and none of the blighters that savour chomping on human flesh.

Credit where it's due, Dave found a perfect spot to make a brew. For good measure, a tiny sandy beach skirted the lochan. Absolute bliss. Our thirst had been quenched, so the next requirement was to cool off. Out with an oversized hankie dunked in the water then tied around the neck; it was getting better by the minute. Now it was the turn of my feet as the boots and socks were discarded.

The bottom of the lochan was surprisingly soft and sandy, with not a pebble or boulder in sight, and the water was shallow for quite some distance. That was a comfort for someone like me who can swim but is a scaredy-cat when it comes to deep water. Dave and Lynne followed after their footwear was cast aside. The water wasn't even cold and we were in Scotland! It really couldn't get any better... or could it?

I stripped off, naked as a jay bird. Once I get a bee in my bonnet, there's no stopping me. Why had I been fiddling and faffing, especially when staying in a tent with no washing facilities? We were alone in the middle of nowhere. I hasten to add that I warned Lynne there could be an eclipse of the sun.

Two minutes later, Lynne turned to Dave and asked if he would be offended if she threw caution to the wind. Of course he didn't mind. It made me chuckle, Lynne asking Dave ... as if he would object!

Poor old Dave was in a real quandary until I asked why he was hesitating; get your kit off, for goodness' sake! He still had his sunhat on until I pointed out that looked rather silly since he was unlikely to suffer heatstroke in the short space of time we were there.

I stayed in the shallows for safety's sake. The chances were pretty slim of some idiot flying a drone in such a remote area, and if anybody was on Ruadh Stac Mor looking down did it really matter? But I confess I kept my ears pinned back for the sound of any low-flying helicopters. Heading for deep water might have been a necessary evil rather than running the risk of traumatising some poor unsuspecting crew!

I can honestly say the skinny-dipping felt the most natural and practical thing to do; no seediness or sleaze whatsoever. An hour later we were fully clothed, back on track to our tent, refreshed in every sense of the word. A truly magical and special time, and one that I doubt I will ever relive.

Beware The Ides of Number 29

GOOD NEWS FROM Martin: the military and political unrest had stabilised in Sikkim. The original plan was back on the table; in fact, the flights were booked. My heart sank with good reason as I read the details: depart Leeds-Bradford Airport early Friday 28th September for Amsterdam; change flights; arrive in New Delhi a tad before midnight on the 28th, and stay overnight at a hotel. On Saturday the 29th, take an internal flight from New Delhi to Bagdogra, before driving to Gangtok.

Dragging myself out of bed at some unearthly hour to go to the airport wasn't the problem, despite the fact that I'm not a morning person. It was the date – 29th September. It was the anniversary of my fall from grace on Bla Bheinn in 2016 and also an anniversary for Dave. Would anybody want to be on the same flight as us if they had insider knowledge?

Every effort had been made to put the ghost of Bla Bheinn to rest in September 2017 – perhaps not completely at rest, but a step nearer to closure. We were having another week on Skye, the same dates as in 2016, and it was a golden opportunity to revisit my nemesis. I might have regained some confidence on the Ledge route with Martin, but I had a date with Bla Bheinn. Strictly speaking, it was more akin to a long-distance relationship. The summit was unnecessary but the gully was integral, albeit the bottom. However, we decided to avoid the 29th at all costs.

On 27th September, Dave and I sat near the base of the gully.

I'd located a specific rock, the one I thought I'd used when waiting for help. I had every intention of walking up into the gulch but wimped out at the last minute. I poured a tot of whisky and raised my 'glass', although to whom or what I'm not sure.

Two days later, Friday 29th September, I was being foolish. I did not want to go out. But superstition is all in the mind and must not be fed – I *must* go out.

Windy conditions had been forecast so the big boys of the Cuillin were out of the question but Marsco, at 736m (2414 ft), would do nicely. Seven of us would be off the summit and on the way back before the weather came in.

True to form, the wind came in. Having lost considerable height, it was merely a brisk breeze that helped our progress and we were at an altitude of only 400m (1312 ft). We were within spitting distance of the glen and safety – but something wasn't right. I heard an ever-increasing roar getting nearer by the second. Sensing something rather unpleasant was about to happen, I assumed the brace/crouch position...

It was over in a flash. All seven of us were blown over in the blink of an eye, including Carl who would be the first to admit to being sturdily built. I was pinned to the ground, unable to move. 'Lynne, I can't move,' I chirped.

'Where are you?' asked Lynne.

'I'm underneath you. You're on top of me!'

Whether it was a mini-tornado or not, that was how I imagined one must feel. Never mind the wind – where was Dave? In times of adversity he was always there looking out for me, but not this time. He was sitting motionless, a few yards below.

I made my way down, half-crawling, half-stooped, listening for that spine-chilling noise for fear of another battering. 'I think I've broken my wrist,' greeted me.

What a caring wife I was. 'You can't have! It's the 29th of September! I knew we shouldn't have come out!' Not a reaction I'm proud of.

The tornado passed, only to be replaced by horizontal, torrential rain. A cocktail of paracetamol, ibuprofen and improvised use of a climbing sling eased Dave's pain. As I drove him to Broadford Hospital, I vowed I would not be going anywhere the following 29th September.

Like it or not, I *would* be venturing out on 29th September 2018. I could only hope that the jinx of the previous two years would not apply to flights.

We Shall Overcome

JUST NINE-AND-A-HALF WEEKS before departure, we received further information from Martin – and it was not what we wanted to hear. He had already spent considerable time, effort and money, along with help from his man in India; they were both eager to make this expedition a reality. However, there were two, possibly three, obstacles in our way.

Firstly, the internal authorities for Sikkim required medical certificates for each of us, signed by our respective doctors, declaring we were fit and able and would not be calling upon them for medical assistance. We had our travel insurance, so this excess paperwork seemed like bureaucracy gone mad. It was something we could have done without, but not insurmountable.

The second, and far more serious, matter related to our intended itinerary: part of the proposed route would not be possible. Martin was required to liaise with the local mountain guide who, unsurprisingly, had his essential 'requirements'. He insisted that numerous porters (whom he happened to employ) must be used and paid at an extortionate rate. Martin was hardly a newcomer to this game; he knew what was required and what a reasonable price was. The demands were unacceptable.

Finally, and just for good measure, there was a possibility that the various military checkpoints could hamper or even prevent our progress.

There had to be a different strategy. Martin compiled an amended itinerary, which included the use of more vehicles than had first been envisaged. Everybody, including Martin, was disappointed. Out of the five of us, Dave and I were the least deflated. We felt certain that Martin would ensure it was a worthwhile trip and, as we had no pre-conceived ideas, it wasn't that important to us exactly where we went. But it was getting close to the visit and that wasn't helping matters, particularly for me who likes everything ship-shape and organised when it comes to planning. I have never booked a last-minute holiday and wouldn't dream of a break where you are clueless about the accommodation. I would make an exception for the Himalaya.

For the next eight days, we spent time obtaining the new medical certificates together with additional photographs for the authorities. This was unsettling; all I wanted was to get the show on the road. On the 1st August, I was extremely unsettled – panic stricken, to be honest.

I was oblivious to the fact that the change in plan had worried others in the group to such an extent that, in the eight days from hearing the news, serious doubts suddenly surfaced.

Martin seemed very understanding and sent a lengthy email explaining more fully how he hoped to handle the situation and that there might be hidden benefits. These would become apparent at a later stage. Within forty-eight hours we were back on track.

My nerves were in tatters; the previous two days had seemed like an eternity as I anxiously awaited replies to messages I'd sent to the group. Each time my phone beeped, I grabbed it to see who had replied. Even Dave, who is far more relaxed than me, was agitated and I began to fear the trip would not materialise. I had to remember this sort of thing came with the territory when organising such an event; perhaps the time had come when I needed to take stock of my unofficial role as an organiser?

The next issue to take me a step nearer to a nervous breakdown was Carl's doctor, who refused to sign the certificate the Sikkim authorities had demanded. This was due to Carl's asthma – and yet Anita, who also had asthma, had no problems with her doctor. Martin managed to tweak the wording so it would be agreeable to both the authorities and Carl's doctor.

There was yet more paperwork that required our attention, this time an application for an Indian visa that was not to be confused with the Sikkim visa. At least this could be completed online but, just when I'd waded through numerous pages of questions, the website crashed. Dave walked by just as I punched the keyboard with both fists. He foolishly commented that my actions would not help matters. The air was blue.

He should know me better by now. I'm not alone in demonstrating my frustration in such a manner. A friend of mine confided that she once pulverised a mouse (thankfully not the four-legged variety) to smithereens when it wouldn't work, swinging it about, holding the wire, smashing it into the desk before it finally died. You know who you are!!!

The idyllic time spent in the Fisherfield area was a distant memory and the enjoyable nervous excitement about the Himalaya trip had been replaced by worries, anxiety and frustration. I no longer found comfort from my faithful friends, the hills and mountains. Their magic had gone and I was worried about possible injury.

While I was concerned about ailments that could jeopardise the expedition, Carl had a better reason to be worried: he had developed leg pain that would not go away. He put it down to a strained muscle and booked in for a few massages. What he actually had massaged I'm not too sure as his leg seemed no better but he was smiling!

By early September, Martin's amended itinerary had been approved theoretically by the powers that be, although we'd not received written confirmation. Our friends outside the group found it hard to comprehend that we still weren't sure where we were actually going. Looking back, I think some kind of safety valve had sprung into action in my little head. I had stopped worrying; in fact, I'd stopped thinking. Wherever we went, whatever happened, it would all work out. This was an expedition and not a holiday.

Two weeks before D-Day, we got the go ahead. We would go to the Sikkim ball and at last I could buy a greeting card. It would be Lynne's birthday while we were away and I wanted to order a personalised card that depicted our whereabouts and would act as a memento. I had a photo of Brumkhangse, the peak that we would climb, so now I could place an order. I hope the Sikkim authorities realise that they delayed production of a birthday card!

The following two weeks were spent practising packing rucksacks. That was easier said than done; for years I've been accustomed to taking as much as I want and throwing my bag in the car. Should I take this fleece or that one; the orange, the purple or the blue? Those trousers or the other pair? My usual philosophy was 'when in doubt, take the lot'. Even going abroad hadn't been too much of a problem. It's not the end of the world to pay for an extra bag and it avoids unnecessary stress. On this occasion it would be different, particularly when the luggage would be on my back most of the time. It didn't help matters that the various airlines had different weight and size restrictions for luggage. Wearing three jackets and three hats all at the same time, pockets bulging with pairs of socks and knickers, would be a solution and one that was acceptable to the authorities. What a crazy carry-on; apologies for the malfunction of my tolerance button.

Detailed planning of what went where, together with a spreadsheet, and I had it sorted. And then another email arrived from Martin with a list of food provisions he would like us to take. Packets of soups, dried potato, cereal bars, fruit cake and salami. Flippin' 'eck! But I remained calm. There were acres of space in our luggage to accommodate the extras – I don't think!

I went back on messaging duties as to who would bring what, and Carl became the 'salami man'. It was suggested he purchased three or four small salamis which would be easier to transport and would stay fresh. Carl does not buy small quantities, particularly when it comes to food. At the first sight of the salami, I wondered if he would be hauled over by the military. The dimensions and shape bore an uncanny resemblance to what I imagine a nuclear missile looks like.

It had also been suggested that we nominate someone to hold the position of treasurer for tipping porters, drivers and staff in general. With the best will in the world, I did not want to take on this task, nor did I want Dave to volunteer as I knew I would become involved. By the same token, I didn't want to be going round in circles waiting for replies; I hadn't got the time, the inclination or the patience for that carry-on. I made an executive decision and asked Lynne if she would oblige. Much to my relief, she said yes. To ease my conscience, she would receive a gift – not quite bribery.

Carl's leg was not improving so he had to bite the bullet and inform Martin. We felt that for Martin to see Carl hobbling into the arrivals hall in New Delhi without prior warning would not be the best way to start the trip. We might well blot our copybooks along the way, but it would be good to start with a clean sheet.

Here is a quick rundown of the itinerary.

Friday 28th September

Depart Leeds-Bradford Airport 06.20 to Amsterdam. Depart Amsterdam 11.40 to New Delhi. Arrive 23.25. Meet Martin in Arrivals. Taxi to Ibis Aerocity Hotel.

Saturday 29th September

Taxi back to airport. Fly New Delhi to Bagdogra. Taxi transfer to Gangtok; stay at Treebo Nettle and Fern Hotel.

Sunday 30th September

Sightseeing and acclimatisation tour around Gangtok and second night at hotel.

Monday 1st October

Complete permit formalities! Taxi to Lachung. Overnight stay at Mandalay Homestay.

Tuesday 2nd October

Walk around Lachung/acclimatisation. Transfer to Victoria Homestay.

Wednesday 3rd October

Leave Lachung. Jeeps partway to Yumthang, walk the remainder to Hot Springs. Camp (acclimatisation).

Thursday 4th October

Walk to Shiv Mandir (base camp).

Friday 5th October

Walk part-way towards advance base camp and return to base camp.

Saturday 6th October–Friday 12th October

Base camp – advance base camp – summit camp – summit Brumkhangse 5635m (18487 ft) – summit camp – base camp.

Friday 12th October

Depart base camp, drive down to Lachung. Overnight at Victoria Homestay.

Saturday 13th October

Drive to Gangtok, Overnight at Treebo Nettle and Fern Hotel.

Sunday 14th October

Drive to Bagdogra. Flight from Bagdogra to New Delhi. Overnight stay Metropolitan Hotel & Spa.

Monday 15th October

New Delhi including sightseeing. Evening meal and transfer to airport for late flight back to UK.

Tuesday 16th October

Arrive back Leeds-Bradford Airport mid-morning.

PART FOUR

Sikkim – The Himalaya

Friday 28th September:
Leeds-Bradford Airport to New Delhi

AT 1.30AM, I was awake and waiting for the alarms to ping. If memory serves me right, we set two alarms just to be on the safe side. Carl had driven from Hull the night before to stay with us. In the next couple of hours, when Wobble became a taxi, I would discover if my instincts were correct that five adults and ten pieces of luggage could fit into a Ford Mondeo. No problem, although whether the front wheels were in contact with the tarmac at all times was debatable. At least I was comfortable as I didn't have to share the driver's seat.

My worries and concerns were a thing of the past. I sang along to 'Rumours' by Fleetwood Mac as we arrived at the airport. The pick-up times I'd given Anita and Lynne worked well; we parked up at precisely the time I had planned.

I removed a sticker from the steering wheel reminding me to put my B2¾ boots on; these couldn't be packed because of the weight allowance. Neither could the bulky down jacket, suitable for minus 15°C, be packed because it would take up too much space. Hopping onto the airport courtesy bus, I couldn't help noticing the pretty flip-flop sandals, painted toenails and strappy sun-tops that one or two of the other passengers were wearing. I smiled, yet I felt no envy for those heading to hot sunny climes – and I also had painted toenails, even if they were hiding in my boots. I had also gone to the trouble of decanting some perfume into a small plastic bottle. It might not be a necessity, but the tent would be so much sweeter smelling of Calvin Klein's 'Eternity'.

While the majority of the passengers queued for the popular holiday destinations, we were first in line for the Amsterdam flight. Nobody was manning the economy desk but the premium/priority desk was staffed and there were no passengers to attend to.

'Could you help me please?' I asked, showing my economy booking confirmation.

'No, you're in the wrong aisle for economy,' came the gruff reply. However, he took a few steps to his right and served me. Such is life.

Rather than our luggage going through on the usual conveyor belt, we were instructed to head for a specific scanning area. The gentleman operating this could not have been more helpful and was most apologetic when he explained that he was required to do a spot check on a certain number of bags. Anita drew the short straw. After all the hours she'd spent packing to ensure specific items were handy, it all went to pot. The check involved a thorough search of everything.

I'd been distracted by sending a last-minute email and turned to see Anita looking flustered. She was trying to explain to the man what the pink gadget was that he'd found in her luggage and was now holding in his hand. We were all rather unkind, laughing and listening to Anita's description of a 'she-wee'. To the uninitiated, it might at first glance resemble a Rampant Rabbit or some other sex toy gone wrong. However, it is a gadget designed for women to have a pee, standing like a man, without having to disrobe. Lynne had kindly bought Anita and I one each; theoretically they were useful, although I had my reservations.

A mild smell of curry drifted from the galleys as we boarded the New Delhi flight. Ninety percent of the passengers were of Asian origin, a reminder that I was heading to a whole new experience. I'd been awake for more hours than I cared to admit but I was not tired. On the approach to New Delhi airport I looked out in anticipation at the street lights and buildings spreading as far as the eye could see. Normally I dislike cities or any built-up areas but this was something quite different: A bird's-eye view by night.

Arriving at any airport terminal normally involves a hike to reach the various checkpoints. New Delhi was no exception. I was curious why such a vast area was carpeted (retro-style brown and orange) which would be difficult to keep clean and would retain the heat, but that was merely a general observation at around midnight in a totally strange place.

Passport control was straightforward but the same could not be said for visa control. It's always difficult choosing which queue to join and we chose the wrong one as far as speed was concerned. We were like lambs to the slaughter, with several innocent people ahead of us.

It proved useful to note the best tactics should we ever get to the front of the queue. I wouldn't have been surprised had one poor lady burst into tears when it came to her turn. She had the wrong papers, which she promptly dropped on the floor. She didn't understand the official and he didn't understand her. Then there was the dreaded electronic fingerprint machine perched on top of the officials' pedestal, which was raised off the floor. Unless you were about six feet tall, it was difficult to place your hand exactly as the man commanded. Should your hand be slightly at an angle, the machine would not recognise your fingerprint. Everyone was willing her to keep her hand straight before the official raised his voice yet again to her. Each time she failed his volume intensified. It evoked memories of *Fawlty Towers*.

I became ever more nervous. Would I be able to manage

Gangtok

Lynne's Birthday Surprise in Gangtok

Seven Sisters Waterfall. *L-R*. Dave, Sue, Lynne, Anita, Carl, Martin

Binodh and Sue in traditional costume (stick to the day job!)

Road chaos on the way to Mangan

Hill-climb Sikkim style

House demolished by a landslide

Mandalay Homestay, Lachung

this onerous task? Without exaggeration, I'd say it took a good thirty minutes before she got the green light. Perhaps now progress could be made – but sadly not. There had been three desks open but now two lots of officials decided to take a tea break. With no warning, they vanished leaving 'Basil'. Had I been back home, steam would have been coming from my ears but, for some unknown reason, I was totally at ease about everything except the thought of the wrath of the official should I fail the machine test.

Anita and Lynne felt that, at the rate we were going, it would hardly be worth going to bed. Considering I'm a lover of a good night's sleep, even that didn't worry me. Finally it was my turn and, by some miracle, the machine said yes. Having watched so many people go through the process, I had sussed it out. Lynne wasn't quite so lucky as the machine totally gave up the ghost and she was told (or rather barked at), 'Just GO!' as he waved his finger aggressively towards the exit.

There were few people around once we reached the baggage carousel. Sweet Fanny Adams was coming through, so I went to investigate. Quite by chance, I espied a mound of luggage tucked away in a corner. We'd been so long with the visa fiasco that our luggage had been taken off the carousel and dumped in a corner. Evidently security about unattended luggage was simply non-existent.

I was enjoying myself. This was a different, unfamiliar world that made me smile. I'm sure seasoned travellers to such places would take it all for granted but I was fascinated, and sometimes naivety brings its own enjoyment.

After exchanging our money for rupees, we finally met up with Martin who had been on an earlier flight and finalised arrangements with Mr Pandey.

We stepped out of the westernised world of air-conditioning and swish retail shops into the heat, humidity and the hubbub of New Delhi. Even the choice of taxis seemed frenetic, as we were surrounded by taxi drivers plying for trade. I stood back and waited for instructions from Martin as to which vehicle I should plonk myself in.

The journey to the hotel was short, but not lacking in entertainment. Tooting of car horns, swapping lanes without indicating, nipping into a space you felt sure the car wouldn't fit was thrilling. Little did I know that what we were experiencing was only a prelude to the real whacky races. The fact it was 1.30am made no difference: I was wide awake and loving every minute of their driving skills.

For some reason, I thought we'd finished with security checks but it was not so. On arrival at the hotel, first the taxi was checked (presumably for explosives) and then our luggage went through a scanner before it was allowed into the building. Lastly, it was our turn to be scanned before entering.

It was 2am and we would regroup at 8am.

Saturday 29th September –
New Delhi to Gangtok

SIX HOURS LATER, we mustered for breakfast, looking out onto a beautiful sunny morning with the temperature already in the low twenties. It could have been difficult to choose what to pick from the buffet breakfast bar, with its array of every imaginable item you could wish for. Remaining healthy was uppermost for me, so two slices of toast with jam would suffice. I couldn't remember if butter was on the safe list or not, so I would do without.

Looking at what the others were having made my breakfast look rather pathetic so I pushed the boat out and ordered a freshly cooked omelette (plain, of course) along with black coffee. I now realise how anal I was. Normally when I'm abroad I enjoy eating local specialities and steer clear of British food, but this was different.

A gentleman called Naveen joined us for breakfast; he would be our cook throughout the expedition and had worked alongside Martin many times in the past. It was obvious Naveen was a lover of food; his rotund midriff gave the game away. Once breakfast was over, which didn't take long in my case, our luggage was taken out to the waiting taxis.

Somebody was there desperately offering assistance for every mortal task, but if we couldn't have managed our own luggage as far as a taxi it would not have been a good omen for what we were about to do. I appreciated that tipping was part and parcel of the culture, and it wasn't the cost since the amounts involved were hardly worth mentioning. The difficulty was adapting to someone wanting to wait on you hand and foot – although, as time went on, I did become rather accustomed to it. Dave reminded me it would not be like that when we went home!

After all the worry about the dimensions of our luggage, we checked in as a group at the airport without any bags being searched and little notice being taken of their weight and size. I had probably worn my B2¾ boots needlessly, but it went some way towards me bonding with them. The internal flight to Bagdogra was under two hours but, as we disembarked from the air-conditioned plane and walked across the tarmac with the thermometer close to 30°C, the boots were exchanged for sandals at the earliest opportunity.

In those two hours, we were transported back in time. The arrivals building reminded me of Yeadon Aerodrome in the 1960s (now Leeds-Bradford Airport). The man-made signage, with little evidence of modern technology and automation, was quite refreshing.

A lady carrying a baby dropped a feeding bottle, which promptly smashed on the floor. It was made of glass. Not being a mum, I am hardly an expert when it comes to baby gear but I'm sure they haven't been made of glass for years.

Amid the mayhem we met up with Binodh, who would be our government liaison officer, a compulsory requirement for our visit. What a charming and polite young man – and someone who would prove to be worth his weight in gold.

We were ushered towards two vehicles, Anita, Lynne, Carl and Binodh in one, Naveen, Martin, Dave and me in the other. The car park seemed chaotic – it was just an area of dust and loose gravel where cars parked in gay abandon. Our car had few features that you would expect to find on today's vehicles, but fortunately had air-conditioning. That's possibly an over-used facility in the UK but here it was a necessity. The seatbelts appeared not to have been used for some time and, as I am a great believer in the adage 'When in Rome do as the Romans' (except when it comes to certain food), I also ignored them. I had gone all that way for a new experience.

Within fifteen minutes of leaving the airport, we realised that the driving in New Delhi had been child's play. This was indeed whacky races but the continual tooting of horns was not a sign of aggression but a means of informing other road users of a car's whereabouts.

Here there was a new spin on switching lanes. We were on a section of road similar to a dual carriageway; if one side was congested, just use the other side irrespective of oncoming traffic. On a 'normal' main road, do whatever takes your fancy – overtake, undertake. The wrong side of the road and grass verges came in handy when there was no room left on the tarmac. I rather like watching car rallying but this beat it hands down – and I was not just a spectator. The tiniest gap on the road and our driver made a beeline for it. The number of times we said, 'Surely not, he won't manage that ... oh yes, he will.'

All this went on amid the other obstacles on the road: cows, dogs, people, bicycles, rickshaws, wheelbarrows and anything else you care to mention. We witnessed an excellent demonstration of the efficient use of space when a motorbike passed us with five people on board: the driver; his wife sitting side saddle wearing a sari and holding a baby; a young child squeezed between Mum and Dad, and an older child straddling the headlamp. No room for crash helmets.

None of this was a total surprise as you see such things in the media when I'd thought what a dreadful carry-on it was. Being in the midst of it threw a whole new light on it. I was relaxed, with not a care in the world, though I didn't envy those in the baking heat with not a breath of air, or packed like sardines in the local buses that squeezed past.

The congestion was particularly bad around the town of Siliguri in West Bengal. Here we saw water buffalo at the edge of a field and the contrast was startling, with the different lifestyles rubbing shoulders.

As we left the lowlands, heading higher in the direction of Gangtok, we left the traffic jams behind. We made better progress, with less ducking and diving, though overtaking on blind bends became the order of the day. It was quite disconcerting but we were into the swing of it surprisingly quickly. It was good entertainment.

The monsoon season had been a little late in leaving the area and had left its mark on the roads. There were signs of recent landslides, together with huge potholes. Parts of the road had disappeared into thin air – or rather hundreds of feet below into the valley – but it made no difference to the overtaking.

We stopped for a quick break to buy a few bananas from a roadside stall. It was fascinating to note several shops all in a row selling exactly the same goods, displayed in exactly the same manner: bananas and crisps, or sometimes crisps and bananas. The crisp packets had been carefully hung up in rows with the bananas dangling at the side. Waitrose, Marks and Sparks, you have been wasting your money all these years on window-dressers producing imaginative layouts; there's no need.

The bananas were tiny but so sweet and tasty; I calculated they were safe. How Dave understood the lady vendor or vice versa, I have no idea. People who speak fluent English sometimes struggle to understand Dave's rather broad Yorkshire accent.

Our first official checkpoint was Rangpo, where we had to present ourselves to the authorities. The building had a large sign outside with wording that left you in no doubt: 'Foreigners

Reporting Office'. With the ceiling fans wafting the humid air around, it felt like we'd stepped back into a 1950s' film as we waited to be seen. Stark furnishings, painted walls and wooden chairs greeted us, along with warnings that listed the consequences should we give any false information.

Dave is an inquisitive soul, and it's in his nature to wander about, opening doors to see what's behind them. He was under strict instructions to stay where he was and to do exactly as instructed! I did not want him carted off and missing out on the mountain.

We were processed quite quickly. Martin and Binodh handed over our documents and passports while we sat in a line in front of the man in charge. He was a man with little to say; he never smiled but he sanctioned our papers.

The next stop was to a nearby teahouse. I tried chai, a milky, sweet, weak tea, a popular drink. It wouldn't be my first choice, but it was acceptable. Martin handed our passports back and, as is usual, everyone sniggered at their friends' passport photos. There was no need for the hysterics when they saw mine: I was having a bad day when the photo was taken and *Prisoner Cell Block H* springs to mind. How cruel people can be.

Walking back towards the cars, I realised we were the focus of the locals' attention. Not in an intimidating manner; far from it – they were smiling and waving at us. How peculiar. I smiled and waved back. One gentleman walked passed me and shook my hand. Even more bizarre.

The road carry-on was now predictable. It was interesting to note that monkeys were happy living alongside the traffic, sitting on some of the rarely-seen crash barriers, with the River Teesta below.

By the time we arrived at the Treebo Nettle and Fern Hotel it was dark but the hive of activity in Gangtok belied the hour. It was a lovely hotel: the rooms were charming, the staff was friendly and the food was excellent. Before we could eat, Martin presented us with an oximeter, a gadget that reads pulse rates and oxygen levels in the blood. Using this would be a daily procedure; altitude-related illness has to be taken seriously and, prevention being better than cure, we would be closely monitored.

There was some leg pulling when I ordered a basic pizza and red wine. They might have laughed but Martin had advised us to ease our way into the local food. Nevertheless, I took Martin up on his offer of a spring roll that was going spare. You can't be too hasty about these things and I was doing my level best not to fall prey to the dreaded squits.

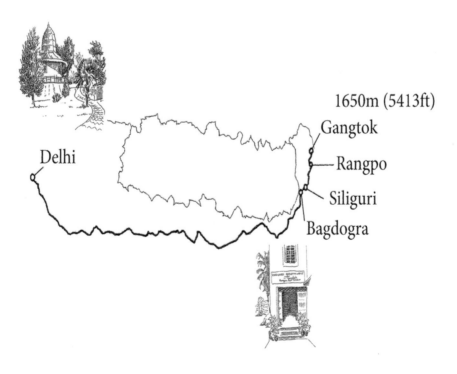

Sunday 30th September – Gangtok

EVEN TAKING INTO consideration the time difference, I'd survived the 29th September without incident. Perhaps the spell had been broken.

I managed to get a reasonable amount of sleep, despite dogs barking and street noise throughout the night. Gangtok certainly didn't sleep; we may have been in a remote part of the world but the noise was reminiscent of a city centre back home.

With space at a premium, buildings were squeezed into tiny spaces and perched on steep hillsides, seemingly with little terra firma for their foundations. Today would be leisurely, with sightseeing and the start of our acclimatisation. Martin was very keen on a controlled programme of adapting to altitude. Gangtok stands at 1650m (5413 ft), a good 300m (1000 ft) higher than Ben Nevis but a darned sight warmer.

Our first port of call was a local Buddhist monastery, a handsome building, immaculately maintained, looking down on Gangtok. Pristine white walls were set off with burnished yellow window frames, scarlet pillars and golden inlay. Perhaps it's places like this that give Farrow & Ball inspiration? Sadly, I'm not the best person to describe architecture, history and religions. I've visited Pompeii, Rome and Venice with Karen, who is entranced by such things; being a total heathen, the history of these places was wasted on me. I felt the life draining out of me when one of the tours lasted three hours.

However, now I was more than happy to play the tourist at the monastery and it gave me an opportunity to show off my new parasol/brolly which I used to give me shade. It was an item mentioned on our kit list but we were told we could buy them once we arrived in India. I didn't want to rely on last-minute shopping, so I'd purchased one at home with a pattern of blue sky and fluffy white clouds. I'll gloss over what it cost and that it was an extra item to squeeze into the rucksack when space was limited.

It was time for a change of religion as we arrived at a Hindu temple. It was a beautiful spot surrounded by trees and shaded grassy areas, with covered walkways decked with bells. Ringing the bells either wards off evil or brings good luck. I chose not to ring them; a few bells would have no bearing on my future.

We had to remove our shoes as a sign of respect and, rather than leaving on my socks, I chose to go barefoot as the locals did. It felt lovely, particularly on the cool soft grass – until I realised a couple of tiny leeches had hitched a lift between my toes. My socks went back on.

Our final visit was to the Himalayan Zoological Park, a nice opportunity to have a stroll and to take a few photos. I became aware of other visitors taking photos; nothing unusual in that but their cameras were aimed at us. To hell with the four-legged wildlife; that received only cursory glances. We were the rare species and were asked where we were from, how long we would be in the area, what we had planned, and wished all the very best.

When it came to explaining where we lived, namely Yorkshire, I mentioned Geoffrey Boycott thinking it might help. My reasoning was that India was a keen cricketing nation. It drew a blank, but I suppose they were far too young to know his name – and why would they be interested in cricket? I was born in

Yorkshire but I'm not hooked on the sport. And I hardly dare say it, but Mum and Dad supported Warwickshire because they came from the Midlands.

We returned to the centre of Gangtok for lunch, where Binodh chose a suitable cafe. Looking at the decor it wouldn't have been my choice, but inside knowledge is everything and the food was lovely. Noodle soup and *momos*, a delicacy on the lines of dumplings but not as stodgy; at last I was venturing outside my comfort zone. Having been fed and watered, we were left to our own devices. Before we went in search of whisky and gin to take to base camp, I discreetly asked Martin if he could buy a celebration cake. It was Lynne's birthday the following day but we would be busy travelling so the surprise would have to be a day early while we were in Gangtok.

That was on the basis we could find our way back to our hotel minus Binodh or Martin. A compass would have been handy. Dave and Carl were ahead and there was a male- female divide about which way to go. The women wanted to regroup and discuss the matter but as far as the men were concerned it was not up for debate. They carried on walking, taking no interest in our opinion. Is it testosterone that brings out the arrogance? We were furious but didn't have the courage to ignore them and go with our instincts. Naturally we were right, yet they still argued that their route was correct even though theirs went the long way around and more or less through somebody's property!

Carl stumbled across some building work in progress; being in the trade himself, he was fascinated. Bamboo scaffolding, workers with no steel-toe-capped boots (actually nothing on their feet), no safety helmets, no high-viz vests and loose wiring dangling perilously close overhead – I've seen tidier spaghetti. Undoubtedly dangerous, but the workers smiled and gave us a wave.

The modern world was literally intermingled with the old. There was spaghetti wiring entwined with what appeared to be banana trees that were vying for position between the buildings. I'm sure Monty Don could tell me what species they were! The shops were a mix of high-street names you would see in any modern European country amongst many traditional stalls. I was undecided whether the modern influence was good or bad. For us it seemed out of place, but was that because it didn't fit the image we wanted to see. The residents of Gangtok might welcome it.

Dave bought a brolly, a lovely tartan design, and revelled in reminding me that it had cost less than a pound, a fraction of what I had paid. We found the drinks shop but failed to find anywhere that sold tonic water. Schweppes might call it Indian tonic water, but nobody had heard of it in Sikkim. Soda water was the substitute; I doubt that gin and soda will ever catch on and it was only slightly more appealing than straight gin.

Back at the hotel would probably be the last opportunity to make use of hot running water, so it was time to wash a few items. There was a restriction on the amount of underwear we could carry to keep the weight down, though I'm sure extra knickers wouldn't have tipped the balance. Washing clothes was easy but drying them was another matter; it was hot but humid so nothing would dry. A wall-mounted fan in the bedroom saved the day. With Dave's ingenuity, my 'smalls' were attached to the fan and merrily blew in the breeze – perfect, but I had to remember them when packing. If I didn't, the cleaners would probably wonder what kind of a ritual this was!

Early evening brought problems. Martin met with the local agent and owner of the local mountain-guiding business. He was a bit of a 'Del Boy', and it became clear that what he said or wanted would happen. There was still a difference of opinion as to the number of porters required; rather more worrying was the additional restrictions imposed by the authorities. I wondered if Del Boy was part of those authorities.

We could cross the army checkpoints only once and that would affect both our trekking and camping plans. Rather than camping, we would be based in Lachung at 2700m (8858 ft) the following two nights, using the local homestays (a version of a B&B), thereby avoiding the army checkpoints. Rather like Monopoly: do not pass Go or proceed to jail! Two vehicles would take us to Lachung the following morning. Del Boy had checked out the road; it was passable but we should expect a bumpy ride. The monsoon season had taken its toll on another road.

On a lighter note, we had a birthday to celebrate. Everyone signed the Brumkhangse card, Martin had done us proud with choice of cake and I'd remembered to pack some candles. Lynne seemed thrilled and genuinely surprised when the waiter came out with the cake. I handed her a little something in the shape of jewellery as an advance thank you for agreeing to be our treasurer – bribery concealed under the guise of a birthday present.

Monday 1st October – Gangtok to Lachung

IT WAS TIME to say farewell to home comforts as we packed our bags for the next stage of our journey. We could leave clothes for laundering ready for our return thirteen days later, and the hotel was happy for us to leave unnecessary items. We repacked accordingly with bags of laundry, bags of items to be left behind and bags to take with us. The last thing we wanted was to muddle them up.

Today would be the last day we were likely to have a signal for contact with the outside world for nearly two weeks. That was a little perturbing in one sense, yet it was charming to return to how things once were. Satellite phones were strictly forbidden and the consequences could result in imprisonment.

Binodh had spent ninety minutes that morning queuing for yet more permits that would allow us through further military checkpoints. We left Gangtok in the same format as before: Anita, Carl, Lynne and Binodh in one vehicle, the rest of us in the other. It was a journey of only sixty miles to Lachung but would take all day; that was hard to grasp at first but several hours later we found out exactly why.

We put on our tourist hats again as we stopped twenty miles north of Gangtok to admire the Seven Sisters waterfall and stretch our legs. As the name implies, the waterfall drops in seven tiers although the top three sections are hidden away. Considering it was a tourist hotspot, the number of visitors was acceptable and a welcoming breeze drifted across the water.

There was a young lady with a tiny stall full of traditional Tibetan costumes in an array of colours. For one hundred rupees she would dress you in the colour of your choice. Why not, if I was going to be a tourist? Let's go the whole hog. I pointed at a garment that took my fancy, only to be told, 'Too small, you need large.' Say it as it is – she would go down well in Yorkshire! There was no malice whatsoever and she spoke English, but not sufficiently to let me down lightly about sizing. They were stunning costumes and a local lady looked elegant and demure in hers; it was a shame the same could not be said about me.

Back on the road again and we were beginning to appreciate the meaning of 'bumpy road'. The potholes and missing sections of tarmac we experienced near Bagdogra were blemishes in comparison. Now the holes were akin to craters; it was rather hairy to drive around a bend to be met by a huge swathe of missing road. And the road was narrow enough without the missing chunks. Several large army trucks, petrol tankers and cars were competing for room with only inches to manoeuvre. Wing mirrors were frequently pulled in; it was either that or lose them, or risk the whole vehicle disappearing into the abyss below.

There were several heart-stopping moments. The adrenaline rush went up a notch but it was still a buzz. Road repairs were an ongoing feature. Families were gathered around piles of rubble and stones, sifting and dividing them according to size, all by hand. The whole family were a gnat's hair away from the traffic and a drop of hundreds of feet. Some children were no more than four years old, and mothers worked with their babies strapped to them. I noted an amputee without crutches and minus a prosthetic, shuffling along on his bottom – yet he too had a smile for us and waved. I had mixed emotions, an uncomfortable feeling of uneasiness and guilt.

Progress had been slow but now we ground to a standstill. The locals were getting out to look, so we followed suit. Further ahead a policeman was waving his arms frantically and blowing his whistle. A small section of the road was on an incline with the top surface a mixture of gravel and mud, just what you would expect to see on an off-road circuit. A petrol tanker was stuck; he could not get enough traction and was attempting to reverse down to a less narrow section to allow other traffic to pass. Meanwhile an army truck was parked up with blocks of wood behind its wheels to prevent it slipping.

The police officer finally brought some semblance of order to the proceedings, halting the downhill traffic to enable the uphill vehicles to take a run at the mudslide. Dave and I opted to wait for our car to complete the hill climb before we hopped back in on the basis that it was front-wheel drive, so less weight in the back might help. It came as a surprise that it wasn't a 4x4.

We'd been taking photos of the off-roading but again I sensed we too were being photographed. I was a little unsure whether I would be frowned upon for wearing shorts. They were far from skimpy, comfy and more akin to 'Don Estelle' shorts. I'm sure Binodh or Martin would have told me if they were not decent.

After the excitement of the hill climb, we relaxed and enjoyed lunch at a rather nice cafe in Mangan. The weather was a little disappointing but I felt sure it was merely a passing shower.

Anita and Lynne had been less than enthusiastic about the roller-coaster ride up to Mangan but we laughed about it, exchanging opinions on driving tactics and enjoying our meal and never noticing the intensity of the rain. Fortunately our drivers and Binodh were rather more diligent; they felt that the sooner we were back on the road the better.

We scurried back to the cars through the torrential rain. Martin was on feather-duster duty and played a crucial part in maintaining our wellbeing as the fan for clearing the windscreen was less than efficient. With the humidity, hot sweaty bodies and the intense rain, it could not cope. The feather duster on the dashboard now made sense; it was the economical optional extra instead of a heated windscreen. Martin dusted down the driver's side, then his own side, then back to the driver's.

By now very few vehicles were on the road, and with good reason. Negotiating the obstacles had become a far more serious affair and it was difficult to judge the depth of the potholes that were full of water. There was little banter as we all concentrated on the road and, as we rounded yet another bend, an uneasy silence descended. A sizeable amount of tarmac had been ripped away. Craters had replaced potholes, there were boulders in the middle of the road and, on the right of us, a steep mountainside was badly eroded and had a miniature river running down. Perhaps we would turn around? No.

There was a small car ahead inching his way across a 200-yard near-suicidal stretch. Had I been driving, I would have waited until he had crossed, giving a clear line of attack before setting off. But I wasn't driving and our man opted for the opposite strategy: tailgate right up the backside of the car in front to chivvy him along. What was even more worrying was that our driver put his seatbelt on!

Now there was no adrenaline buzz; I had stepped over the line to sheer terror as the car in front stalled, seemingly stuck in a hole. His reversing lights came on but, as we tried to reverse, the rear end of our car started to slide ever closer to the vertical drop.

For fear of making a drama out of a crisis, I opted to simply state a fact. As I grabbed Dave's knee, holding on for grim death, I announced, 'I'm frightened.' Dave would normally have commented but he said nothing. Nobody spoke; I suspect

I'd said what everyone was thinking.

I looked up to my right to see large pebbles tumbling down the mountainside; oh my God, the banking was surely going to give way. My escape plan had been to walk across but, looking at the speed of the water coming down, that was no longer an option. We could feel the ever-increasing force of the water against the wheels of the car. We couldn't go forward and we dared not go back. For a few seconds I honestly believed it was curtains for us.

By some miracle, the car in front started to make headway and it was our turn in the cavernous hole. There was an eerie silence, bar the sound of Martin dusting furiously to ensure we could at least see how and where we were about to meet our maker.

We made it! Thank goodness it wasn't the 29th September; maybe I should have rung those bells at the temple! The road improved but we passed a partially demolished house and discovered it had been swept away only that morning. We were one of the last vehicles to get through; the 'suicide stretch' was closed, hit by a landslide.

The rain had stopped by the time we reached Lachung and the Mandalay homestay. It was a lovely little B&B run by a lady and her two daughters and, with much relief, we met up with our friends. Our room felt luxurious with its en-suite bathroom, something I didn't expect. Lynne and Anita weren't quite so lucky. Their beds felt damp, verging on wet, so they opted to sleep on top in their sleeping bags. We ate in an outhouse, extremely basic but the food was lovely and cooked in front of us. I watched in wonder at how such a tasty meal could be made with the most simple of equipment.

Today was Lynne's birthday, one she would never forget after the near-death experiences on the road. To be born and die on the same date would be a tidy affair when it comes to paperwork, but not when you have many more years left in you. It was a thought I once had in Scotland on my birthday. The weather was dire, we were on a summit in a whiteout with a gale blowing and, in rather a matter-of-fact way, I thought that if I died on my birthday everything would be ship-shape and organised. That's just me and my twisted thoughts; I do have a black sense of humour which Dave struggles with at times.

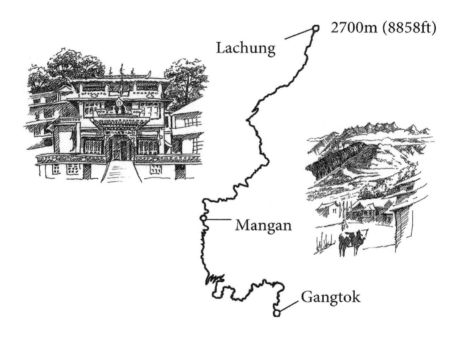

Tuesday 2nd October – Lachung

IT WAS A very civilised start to the day when tea was brought to our rooms. I suspected it could have been a sweetener when we discovered there was another change to the plans that would test our skills when it came to packing and deciding what should go where. Firstly, we were to change accommodation, moving a spit's throw down the road for one night. One of our drivers had a brother who happened to run a hotel and so, with some reluctance, Martin agreed. I got the impression his hands were tied because where we were was perfect.

Our luggage needed splitting between items that could go straight to base camp in a vehicle and things we'd need the following day for an interim camp adjacent to some hot springs. As I write, it sounds a simple procedure but for some unknown reason it tested all our brain cells.

We had our first proper outing to look forward to that morning, a walk up to the high meadows above Lachung with the aim of reaching an altitude of 3100m (10170 ft). Binodh, our guide, met us wearing immaculate white trainers that appeared to have just come out of a box. Admittedly none of us were wearing the dreaded B3 boots, having been told that for the majority of the expedition approach shoes would suffice – but white trainers? I opted for approach shoes, while the others chose everyday walking boots. Within minutes of leaving the village we encountered mud, yet Binodh's footwear remained clean. Floppy sunhats were also part of our uniform, although that was somewhat short-lived when the mist descended and once again we were sampling typical Scottish weather.

I'm sure we looked nothing like budding mountaineers in training for encounters with mighty peaks, crevasses and glaciers. Martin also ribbed us about our Mickey-Mouse rucksacks. Dave and I had stumbled across some foldaway rucksacks in a local shop back home. We needed to keep weight to a minimum but wanted to avoid carting our large sacks around until we had to so, Mickey Mouse or not, the foldaway ones would do nicely. Martin may have laughed at the start of our trip but I think he saw their potential by the end of it.

We passed many white prayer flags interspersed with coloured flags lining a ridge onto the meadows. Had Lynne been writing this book she could have explained their significance, but this is me. I could Google them but you might be suspicious of the new, studious style. Walking through the pastures amongst grazing cattle was rather like the Yorkshire Dales except for the height we were at and the fact that prayer flags are few and far between around Malham Cove.

Martin seemed happy once we reached 3100m (10170 ft) so then we did an about-turn and went back for a late lunch at the Mandalay homestay. It was a crying shame we had to move on from the green-painted chalet where the lady grew her own organic vegetables, surrounded by apple orchards. A few chickens wandered about and the occasional cow passed by heading for the night-life in Lachung.

The family kitten took a shine to me. He (or she) was a cute little thing and I gave it my attention even though I'm not a cat lover. I was aware of the potential rabies risk but it seemed healthy and well-cared for.

We were like the lost tribe of Israel as we left the Mandalay and wandered down the road to our new abode with a few of our worldly possessions in our arms. My passport photo might look like I'm a resident of *Prisoner Cell Block H*; the establishment we moved to could have featured in the same series. A functional rectangular block with an unfinished extension perched on top, the building had no charm or character. Whether the foundations could withstand an extension was debatable.

Our bedroom was large, and there was an en-suite bathroom that had seen better days, but the bedding left a lot to be desired. Ignorance is bliss so I chose not to investigate too closely and took out my sleeping bag. The exposed wiring to the light switch was more than shabby chic, so the headtorch was at the ready as backup. I think that was the only time I whinged and later I regretted it, reminding myself that no matter what was thrown at me during the expedition I would remain positive. My days of worrying were over once I left Hellifield.

Lachung was a mish-mash of traditional lifestyles. Many families grew their own produce – and then we would go around a corner to see modern buildings with the now-familiar spaghetti wiring strung across the road. It seemed a sizeable, thriving community, cut off from the outside world.

We met one of the locals who was acting very strangely. I'm not saying he was on drugs, but his mannerisms were decidedly unconventional. He decided to chat to Dave, and I felt for both parties. Dave's people skills came to the fore. He walked backwards in the middle of the road, with his hands on his hips and looking at the rest of us, saying loudly, 'Does anybody know what he's on about 'cos I don't.' I carried on walking.

We took in another monastery. Dave and I had never visited so many religious buildings in such a short space of time – and there wasn't a bolt of lightning to be seen!

Our bedroom left a lot to be desired but where we ate was far more welcoming. When we asked if we could buy a few drinks, the lady of the house opened up her other sideline: a shop. The choice was beer or Bacardi Breezers. Not being a lover of beer or lager, I opted for two of the latter. I was in luck, but the same could not be said for Lynne and Anita who chose beer: they were allowed just one bottle between them, while the men could have as many as they wished. Women drinking too much alcohol was frowned upon, and a bottle each was deemed as excessive. I'm fairly sure the men discreetly shared theirs.

Before we ate and drank, Martin had taken our health check readings and written the results in his little black book. It all made absolute sense and by the end of the trip we would know one another in ways we never had before.

A few Asian visitors to Lachung ate at the Vic. I noted that no cutlery was offered when their food was served; they ate in the traditional way, using their hands. Thankfully we were given cutlery, though Dave would have happily coped using his hands! If it was a case of eat or go hungry, I would too – and of course wild camping has its own rules – but I was brought up to use a knife and fork and sit at a table. I still dislike the habit of eating with only a fork. I'm certainly not from the upper echelons of society, far from it. I was brought up in a simple semi-detached on the outskirts of Bradford but certain habits never leave you.

We finished off the evening with a card game, which was only slightly more complex than Snap, using cards relating to Munros. The boss seemed less than impressed, even though he won; the game did not require enough skill for his liking. It suited me – didn't he know that straightforward can be enjoyable?

Wednesday 3rd October –
Lachung to Yumthang

DAVE AND I had been lazy the previous evening and dismissed the idea of taking a shower. The bathroom wasn't particularly enticing but this morning was our last opportunity to have a shower for many days to come.

Rather than a shower, I would call it a jug-and-bucket dunk. You filled the bucket with hot water from a tap on the wall then used the jug to scoop water from the bucket to throw over yourself. I suppose you could throw over the full bucket and have done with it, but the enjoyment would be short-lived. Perhaps it was a prototype of a wetroom?

Dave was well pleased with the end result and now it was my turn. Marvellous: he'd used all the hot water and there wasn't time to wait for the boiler to heat another tankful. Thank goodness it was only one jug of cold water at a time – a bucket of cold water in one drenching might have been a step too far.

Then our bad planning came to light: we had taken one large towel to share and Dave was the first to use it, getting it so wet it was neither use nor ornament for me. Travel towels are a far cry from soft fluffy towels you might have at home! He apologised and I was surprisingly forgiving, but I still needed to dry myself. I used a T-shirt that I'd been wearing for the previous two days. It was useless for reaching my back so Dave stepped into the breach. There I was, arms in the air, as if I was guiding an aircraft taxiing into its gate, at the same time being leathered down as you would a car. He was very rough but I was clean and warm from the friction burns!

Au revoir to the Vic as our cars took us towards Yumthang. We were walking the final six miles as part of the acclimatisation regime. The journey to our drop-off point was enlightening as we read the various road signs: '*Stop gossip, let him drive*', '*Sorry shooting stones*' and, outside one of the many barracks we passed, '*God have mercy on our enemies because we won't*'.

One particular checkpoint had a far more serious feel to it than others we'd encountered. There was a sign with a whole list of prohibited goods and behaviour, and a reminder that punishment and fines would follow should you disobey. Understandably no photography was permitted but, interestingly, no plastic bottles were allowed into the area. There were no smiles from the guards on duty, but Binodh's many permits and paperwork received the sign of approval.

I recall seeing either an officer or an NCO looking immaculate in his uniform and wearing a turban. Impeccable and yet a formidable sight; you wouldn't have wanted to cross swords with him. There is something about a man in uniform – they look so smart – but I wouldn't be waving at this particular man!

Having been on our best behaviour, we were beckoned through the barrier and driven on to our drop-off point. Under Binodh's supervision, most of our gear would be taken by car to our interim campsite alongside the hot springs.

Before he left us, he was at pains to stress to us all – but particularly Martin – the importance of remaining on the road. Under no circumstances were we to take shortcuts. 'Sir, you must stay on the road.' If the army caught us, we could be shot. That seemed a good enough reason to conform.

I think the drivers struggled to understand why we chose to walk when they were going to exactly the same place in the car. They didn't have acclimatisation to take into account.

The original plan, or rather one of the many original plans, was to head straight to base camp at a height of 3915m (12844ft). Martin wasn't keen because it would have meant a big jump in altitude in the region of a 1000m (3000ft plus), more than he would have liked, hence the hot springs interim camp at 3600m (12000ft).

We were walking on a road but it was pleasant, with pine trees and rhododendron bushes lining our way. Unfortunately, for some unknown reason, Martin dislikes rhododendrons with a passion so it wasn't just us that had the knack of rattling his cage: the foliage could too! It just so happened we were visiting an area proud of its thirty-eight varieties of rhododendrons.

I lost count of the number of army trucks that passed us. Each time they slowed down and smiled, and I felt at ease waving to them as they appeared to be squaddies with a less-threatening, albeit less-attractive, demeanour than the officer/NCO.

All was fine until a car passed by and promptly slammed on its brakes. It ground to a halt in the middle of the road and five young men jumped out. Panic: what had we done wrong? Were we about to be mugged? Quite the contrary; they had stopped to say hello, shake our hands and ask if they could they take a photo of us! I felt like a celebrity. Had I been forewarned, I might have found room in my rucksack for my make-up bag.

My spirits were high as I trolled along, chatting away, unlike Carl who was beginning to show signs of breathlessness.

Before arriving at our destination, I had conjured up a romantic picture of what these hot springs would be like: peace and tranquillity; pools of water sparkling in the sunshine, surrounded by green meadows and silver pines with a backdrop of mountains. We crossed a bridge spanning the Lachung Chu river, festooned with prayer flags, to access this mini paradise. I was wrong on all counts except the meadow.

The sun was hidden by low cloud, which in turn concealed

the mountains. There was not a pool of water to be seen, as the hot springs were inside a building and the water ran into a large bath. As for having the place to ourselves, it was obviously a popular spot for the locals to visit who wanted to take a mini-holiday.

Binodh and Dawa, one of the porters, were there to greet us. They had erected our tents adjacent to a couple of buildings where a group happened to be staying while on a retreat. Not what I had in mind!

Although we were camping, there were toilet facilities in a nearby building. This was an unexpected luxury so we went to view this hidden delight. I won't beat about the bush; it was crap in every sense of the word. The smell hit you as you opened the door. It was a 'drop toilet', a ceramic surround for your feet as you squatted over a hole. That wasn't the issue, it was the state it was in. Squatting without any support plays havoc on my thigh muscles but I would not have dared put my hands on that floor to steady myself. It was advantageous not to be able to see properly, as I came out retching; I would certainly be making my own alternative arrangements. After our guided tour of the toilet, my bottle of anti-bacterial hand gel stayed with me wherever I went, rather like a child refusing to go anywhere without their teddy bear.

After a quick drink and bite to eat, we wandered down to the river. We saw smoke billowing from our campsite – it was a ritual of our neighbours who lit a fire to please the mountain gods. Keep lighting the fires, I say. I would not dismiss any belief after my *faux pax* with the bells!

The men chose the muddier path and went out of sight while the women went on the opposite, and much wider, bank with a more substantial path. We were saving ourselves for the mountain. The river was wide and fast flowing with an abundance of 'those' shrubs along the riverbank. It reminded me of the Lake District, particularly because it was raining.

The men must have marched on at a pace because they were back before us, but I'd found a potential venue to dig my own little loo hidden amongst the trees, with fresh air and far enough away from the river. It would mean a good five-minute walk but that was a small price to pay. Thankfully, Dave and I had brought our own mini fold-up 'shit shovel'. There will be more about our toilet procedures later!

Dave seemed overly pleased to see me when we arrived back at camp. He had been looking for me and wandered into the hot-springs bathing area, quite a small steamy room, calling, 'Sue, are you there? Anita, Lynne, are you there?'

There was no reply, then the steam cleared to reveal several naked ladies in the water who seemed totally at ease with Dave's presence. At the same time, a man ran towards Dave, waving his arms and shouting that the bath was a women-only session! It's a wonder he wasn't arrested. My back is turned for a minute and he gets himself into trouble.

The drama over, we went into the mess tent for a meal. Some of the ladies chose to come and say hello; was it because we were foreigners or had they come to see Dave?

Time for bed and off to our respective tents. Binodh and Dawa were sleeping in a mess tent that was already in place, Carl and Martin were in one of our tents, and Dave was the lucky man who would be keeping an eye on the women.

It was a little frustrating when I used my headtorch during the night as, just for a few seconds, it developed a mind of its own and flashed on and off.

Thursday 4th October –
Yumthang to Shiv Mandir/Base Camp

WE WOKE TO another cloudy day. Unfortunately, the clouds were not confined to the sky above; there was thunder near the tent itself. Neither Anita nor Lynne had managed a wink of sleep. A dog, who had visited us the previous day, had barked on and off throughout the night.

Dave and I were oblivious to the disturbance. Some of the locals, who were staying in the adjacent building, had been hawking and clearing their throats; again, this was news to us. There was a small leak in the brand-new tent and it just happened to be close to Anita and Lynne. Finally, to put the tin lid on it, there was the small matter of Mr and Mrs Pugh getting up throughout the night for a pee. Four times in total. It was a pity we couldn't co-ordinate our pee stops but my bladder didn't know what Dave's bladder was thinking.

It was a bit of a faff: on and off with footwear and unzipping the tent seemed rather loud to light sleepers. Apparently the insomniacs had devised a cunning plan during the night: one would catch the barking dog and the other would kill it. I believe that Dave and I were also on the hit list, if the mood was anything to go by!

The imaginary knife that would have killed the dog would have been handy to cut the atmosphere in the campsite. The word 'tetchy' springs to mind. I think the fact that Dave and I were quite perky probably exacerbated the situation.

Off I toddled, implement in my hand, to seek out my own personal loo stop and far enough away from the black looks. I adhered to the policy that no toilet paper should be left behind; we put used paper in nappy sacks to be burnt later. Just remember to keep the used nappy bags separate from everything else.

The tents were dismantled and left for Binodh and Dawa to transport to base camp by car. We set off along the banks of the river before passing through yak meadows and then back to meet the road. The evidence of old landslides was unbelievable: it looked like half a mountain had broken away, taking with it everything in its path. It was Armageddon, spread over a region of 500 metres, with boulders larger than houses and little sign of any life.

The weather wasn't lightening the mood; the brollies came out as it started to rain. I sensed chuntering from certain quarters so kept my distance and decided against commenting on the fact the weather was not dissimilar to Scotland, and at least the rain was warm.

Binodh and Dawa passed us, giving a rather cheeky wave from the comfort of a vehicle. I have to confess I've always dismissed walking with a brolly but it did have an advantage: I could keep dry without the need for extra clothing. There was a time, many years ago, when Dave led guided walks in the Lake District and a gentleman we'd never seen before arrived with a golfing brolly. Dave told the poor man in no uncertain terms to leave it on the coach. No, it wasn't Nicholas Crane!

Carl was looking a little worse for wear, not through lack of sleep but because of the altitude. His breathing was laboured and his eyes showed signs of puffiness. Fortunately base camp wasn't far and lunch was waiting for us when we arrived.

Our first impressions were favourable. The tents were concealed in the shrubbery and dotted about in a clearing.

The Vic, Lachung

Festooned bridge, Yumthang valley, leading to a debatable mini-paradise

'Singing in the Rain' heading towards Yumthang

Dawa modelling the latest climbing footwear!

Log bridge to negotiate shortly after leaving base camp.
Helmets worn as Martin feared a Great Gully re-run!

Dawa and Dave with the Yorkshire flag at Advance Base Camp

View from Advance Base Camp on the rare occasion we had visibility

Accessing the glacier

Our only neighbours appeared to be a few horses. The outline of the surrounding peaks was difficult to distinguish as the clouds chose to keep that spectacle for another day.

The porters had dug a trench toilet and there was the luxury of a tiny tent for privacy; there was even a toilet roll hanging up. The engaged sign was to place a trekking pole or ice axe outside the tent. You then placed a shovel of soil over the evidence and the paper went in a bag. It was a hundred times better than the previous facilities. My apologies to those of you who are fully aware of the whole toilet business in these places, but there might be somebody reading this who is unaware of such matters. Drop toilets and trench toilets were new additions to my vocabulary. At one time, I thought Armitage Shanks were the only ones on offer.

There was a change in sleeping arrangements: Anita and Lynne would have a two-man tent; Carl would be in with Dave and me, and Martin would have the luxury of his one-man tent. He needed a little privacy away from us lot for some of the time.

Now we were at base camp I had a better understanding of the staff we had. Binodh, our liaison officer, was a proficient climber but he was there in his officer role. He hadn't been employed under any other banner, was recovering from an illness and couldn't climb even if he had wanted to. Naveen was our cook for the days at base camp, together with his helper. We had three porters: Dawa One, Dawa Two and Pashthung. It was Lynne who helped with that information; she even remembered the names of the different drivers we had throughout the trip.

Carl discovered his bottle of hand gel (a large bottle of course, as it was Carl's) was, in fact, liquid soap. We took it in turns to allow him a blob of ours. Martin's little black book appeared along with the health-measuring gizmo. Typical of Dave: he was Superman with perfect readings and the altitude had no effect on him whatsoever. Unfortunately Carl's readings were far from ideal. Other details were logged, all pertinent to our wellbeing, but it was amusing when we were asked in turn about our bowel movements, how often and what was the consistency! I was happy to answer, but I sincerely hoped proof would not be required. I draw the line at some things.

The whisky and gin came out to accompany our meal. Martin was as keen as anyone for a tipple. Gin and soda would take some getting used to but beggars can't be choosers and I was happy to drink my whisky straight. Sitting on the floor of his kitchen mess tent, Naveen conjured up some marvellous dishes: soups, curries, pasta, omelettes and even chips.

The card game was abandoned but I offered to play some music from my phone. Folk seemed to like the idea, although Dave was less enthusiastic. I appreciate ballads and he doesn't. (This is the man who regards Jimi Hendrix as ideal background music whilst having a meal!) I don't think there is anything wrong with Celine Dion but, after playing one particular track, 'Think Twice', several times, I relented and changed the mood.

Time for bed – but 'the song of Sikkim' was still playing in my head.

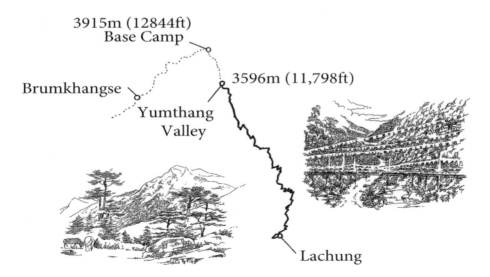

3915m (12844ft)
Base Camp

3596m (11,798ft)

Brumkhangse

Yumthang
Valley

Lachung

Friday 5th October – Base Camp – 4400m Dumping Area – Base Camp

TEA WAS SERVED at 5.30am followed by breakfast at 6.30am. Each morning we were treated to a cuppa while we were still in our sleeping bags.

Carl looked no better, so Martin started him on a course of Diamox, a drug that can help with altitude sickness. At this stage it could, at best, only stop further deterioration. For it to be as efficient as possible, it should be taken continually and before reaching high altitudes as a preventative measure. It can mask symptoms, so the choice about whether to take it beforehand seems to be a chicken-and-egg situation. We'd been given plenty of information and the choice was ours. None of us chose to take it as a preventative measure.

Rather naively, I once thought that altitude sickness equated to nausea and headaches. I was ignorant of the far more worrying issues of fluid on the brain and lungs that can result in death. Altitude sickness has to be taken seriously. I'm not a qualified medic but, if I'm not mistaken, any altitude above a good 3000m (10000 ft) may start to affect the body, particularly if you spend a prolonged time at such a height.

Our objective for the day was to climb to a height of 4400m (14435 ft) and deposit some gear in readiness for the following day before retracing our steps back to base camp at 3915m (12844 ft). This was another part of the acclimatisation, but at least it would be the start of the route that would ultimately take us to our goal, our mountain Brumkhangse.

Meanwhile, we were asked to gather items that we wouldn't need until we were at advance base camp (ABC.) Three porters would be carrying this directly to ABC. I was getting feather-legged about what I needed immediately, what could be stashed away at the 4400m dumping ground and what could go to ABC. I needed a spreadsheet as the altitude was playing havoc with my ability to think!

The entourage left base camp and passed through a small, temporary, shack-type village where employees of the Border Roads Organisation lived during the summer months. Tending those roads would be a job for life! Basic accommodation was a generous term for their living quarters: these glorified tin sheds made the properties in Lachung appear positively slick.

A few hens clucked alongside unhealthy-looking dogs. The families seemed happy and fascinated by us. Word spread and, one by one, they came out to wave to us. Our three porters led the way, with one carrying a huge machete to clear a way through the dense undergrowth and rhododendrons. That would put a smile on Martin's face! Within minutes they were forging ahead carrying huge loads, and all they had on their feet were wellies.

A rather nice log bridge took us over a full stream. Holding hands, we shuffled across in formation. Because of my track record of falling down gullies, Martin had us wearing helmets as we then negotiated a small boulder field. A little over-cautious, I thought, but I was the last person who could comment.

It was very much an alpine plod as the lack of oxygen snatched away your breath – except for Superman and the boss. The pine trees we left behind were replaced by bilberry bushes but there were still plenty of Martin's favourites (I'm fed-up with typing rho… Why couldn't he dislike roses?).

As we gained height and the way ahead became more

apparent, Martin took his leave and upped his pace to meet up with the porters. He wanted to ensure they set up the advance base camp in the correct place. We Himalayan fledglings were trusted to continue up the ridge to 4400m and find a suitable place to offload some gear.

When left on our own, the men tended to take command. That was acceptable in itself, as they had more experience under their belts. They worked together to a certain degree, but there was room for improvement when it came to communication between the two of them.

It was another matter when it came to listening to the females' opinion. Admittedly you need a leader because the 'committee system' is quite inefficient and rarely works, but I think they could have taken us more seriously a little more often. Occasionally I commented that 'we' needed to work as a team. 'Yes, Sue,' they said, as they carried on walking!

The gear was dumped and now we caught a glimpse of the terrain that awaited our company the following day. It was shrouded in mist but we got a hint of the scale. It was slightly sobering, though poor weather makes everything more intimidating. I remained positive.

The difference in speed between Martin and the porters and we fledglings was considerable. They caught us up on the homeward stretch after they'd gone considerably further and higher than us.

Back at base camp, tea in our tent seemed like a good idea until I spilt mine over myself and my sleeping bag. The sleeping bag took priority when it came to mopping up since I couldn't afford for that to be wet. Thank goodness I had a spare top. The minimalist theory is all well and good but it leaves no room for accidents. That was why Anita, Lynne and I had taken some disposable knickers as back-ups; the idea of 'accidents' along those lines didn't bear thinking about.

Someone had visited Binodh that afternoon whilst we were away; an angry army officer had seen our camp from the road and was less than pleased, demanding to know who we were and what was going on. Binodh showed him the various permits and, after a few uncomfortable moments, the officer agreed we could stay. We gathered that the heavy military presence and fragile tolerance of visitors was due to the Chinese border being only a few miles away. I'm sure if the officer had met us, he would have quickly realised we posed no security threat whatsoever!

Our daily medical notes were updated as we enjoyed a drink together. Sometimes I can anticipate what Dave's next move or words might be and cut him off at the pass. Sadly, I'm not foolproof.

Dave has two false teeth on a plate, something not uncommon, but how many people would suddenly decide the best way to refresh them would be to dunk them in a cup of tea in front of everyone else? His defence was that he was improvising as there were no proper facilities. Fine, but not in the company of others! I was not best pleased. He was shown the yellow card and, should there be a repeat offence, it would be the red card. Was he worried? Of course not.

They say we have evolved since caveman days but I sometimes have my doubts. Having said that, suave and sophisticated doesn't do it for me. Perhaps it's just as well!

Saturday 6th October – Base Camp – Advance Base Camp

I QUICKLY REALISED that mountain guides operating in the Himalaya have to be prepared to expect the unexpected on a daily basis.

Martin had a major obstacle to solve. None of the porters were high-altitude porters and, although one was willing to help, he did not have the required clothing or gear. Everyday clothes and a pair of yellowy-gold wellingtons would not pass muster. Martin had a few spare items, including crampons, and Anita's lightweight boots that she'd used for low-level walking, more or less fit Dawa. It was those – or we'd be carrying everything ourselves and, with the best will in the world, that would have been an impossible task.

It appeared that Del Boy had pulled a fast one. Unless I'm wrong, he had charged Martin for a high-altitude porter when that was not what he'd supplied. We were in the middle of nowhere, though, so could only work with who and what was available.

Generally, I'd been remarkably laid back about everything, accepting whatever situation was thrown at me – which certainly isn't my default setting. But had I been too complacent?

The next hiccough was my B2¾ boots. I had mistakenly sent them up to advance base camp but I would need them once we reached the snowline. Martin didn't seem particularly worried and joked I might have to be dragged up on a rope if I couldn't keep my footing! I was about to find out exactly how good approach shoes were.

This was the last time we would have any real contact with the outside world for six days and our chance of meeting anyone was highly unlikely. That was quite a serious yet exciting proposition in view of the environment we were entering. This was a true expedition, full of unknowns, and one of the main reasons why I chose it in preference to a conventional tour.

We followed the same format as the previous day, with three porters leading the way, but only Dawa would stay with us. Hopefully we would find where we had dumped the gear. We'd had the sense to mark the spot with several rocks perched on top of the boulder so, unless some beast had demolished the pile during the night, we should be able to locate our goodies.

More snow had fallen during the night and the snowline had crept down the mountain. Soft wet snow: bloody marvellous when I hadn't got my boots. I was grateful I had some waterproof socks and that the technology seemed to have improved. I once regarded them as a waste of money because your feet still got wet and they weren't comfortable.

While I am on the sock business, a tactic I once used on the Isle of Skye (on a Munro by the name of Sgùrr Mhic Choinnich) was put to the test again. Wearing socks over boots gives a surprisingly good grip on slimy, slippery rock but it's only a short-term fix before they wear out.

There was a considerable stream to cross en route to advance base camp. With balance not being my strong point, the rocks I had to teeter on to cross the stream were wet and slippery, tricky with boots on let alone shoes. An extra pair of socks that I'd smuggled under the Moran radar saved the day. They worked perfectly. I reached ABC in one piece and without the aid of a rope. My approach shoes had excelled themselves as we hit an altitude of 4540m (14895 ft) but they were not to be recommended; my feet were decidedly chilly and I was actually pleased to be reunited with my B2¾ boots.

Having done their job, two of the porters returned to base camp while Dawa remained with us. We implemented a new combination for sleeping arrangements: for the first night, Dave and I would be in the blue tent on our own, Dawa would have the orange tent and the remaining four would be in the yellow tent. I've decided rather than referring to three-man, two-man, one-man-and-his-dog tent, I shall refer to them by colour.

We were well placed for spectacular views but at that moment it could have been another day in the Scottish Highlands with the clag (mist) touching the top of the tents and ample soft deep snow. The occasional boulder poked its black nose out, whilst the ground and sky blended into one. I quickly became disorientated as to which direction we had come from, and could only just make out the silhouettes of Dave and Dawa busy digging a trench toilet in the snow.

Our evening medical showed the women's stats had dropped. 'Batman' and 'Robin' were perfect but Carl's had taken a serious dip. An early night was on the cards as Martin hoped to start at 4am the following day.

It was a treat for Dave and me to have a tent to ourselves and lovely to have more space; more to the point, our sleeping habits didn't disturb the light sleepers. It had started to prey on my mind and I was increasingly concerned about what we could do to reduce the number of our night-time forays. I fell asleep before I found a solution.

Sunday 7th October – Advance Base Camp – 'Hidey Hole' – Advance Base Camp

THERE WAS MOVEMENT outside the tent: Martin was knocking snow off our homes. A good four inches had fallen and, not knowing how much more might fall, it was a precautionary measure to avoid the tents collapsing under the weight of the snow. That would be damned inconvenient!

According to Lynne it was 2.30am when all this happened. Martin had asked Dave what the reading was on his altimeter. The pressure was decreasing and that indicated the weather was taking a nose dive, therefore we would not rise at 4am; 8am would be the next wake up call. I was vaguely aware of these goings-on but it would take more than that to wake me from my slumbers.

Totally out of character, our leader allowed us a leisurely breakfast without keeping an eye on the clock. I have it on good authority that the plan was to have a short walk later that day but I confess I hadn't a clue what had been planned or said. There's a total void in my memory library and a blank in my scrawled notes. It's immaterial, as a revised plan came to the fore.

Suddenly there was a sense of urgency; we needed to make tracks and head in the direction of the glacier to perform another gear-dumping ceremony before the next snowstorm came in. A roaming Yeti would have had a heyday pilfering equipment. To be on the safe side, I draped the Yorkshire flag over our tent. It was intended for the summit but there was no harm in giving it an airing – and it might have pleased a passing beast if he hadn't had Lancastrian connections!

After quickly packing the rucksacks, we were off again. It was hard work walking through the snow but we had it easy compared to Martin, who was breaking trail. Being the first to make footsteps in virgin snow may sound attractive but it's incredibly hard graft; throw in the altitude and it's worse. Following on behind was much easier – easier still for those who had slept.

I detected a little irritability from Lynne, who was suffering from lack of sleep that translated into frustration when she packed her rucksack and got flustered. I think high altitude suited me; I've never been so accepting of my situation. I wasn't disappointed at the initial lack of views due to low cloud, and the clouds were kind enough to break for a while to give us our first view of our surroundings. Huge peaks, white mountains and inky black buttresses competed for our attention, some near, some far away, many never having lost their virginity to mankind. A reward like that worked wonders for morale.

We found a hidey-hole, our treasure was stashed, and it was time to lose height then regain it to get back to ABC. Great fun going down to go up again, to then go down, to go up and so on and so forth.

Carl said very little. Not only was he struggling with his breathing but his leg was causing problems. It was painful and the effort of constantly lifting it through the deep snow was doing him no favours.

I felt quite perky when we arrived back at ABC, so I popped back down a few hundred yards to collect water from the glacial stream to make a cuppa. I might have 'popped' down but I staggered back up with litres of water a little less perkily.

As an old Yorkshire saying goes, 'Trouble at t'mill'. Dawa

announced to Martin that he was going back to base camp and wasn't going any further. It was one of those tense moments when we didn't know what would happen next. There was not a cat in hell's chance that we could carry everything unaided.

Martin was polite but firm, repeating, 'I am the boss and I will say what is happening.'

I pretended not to hear, fearing Dawa's reply and dreading the consequences. It all seemed surreal: there we were in a hostile environment with the potential for industrial action on our hands. I'd never imagined such a situation. Dawa stayed, but the sooner we moved higher the better before he ignored Martin and threw in the towel.

We gathered together for our evening meal. I was impressed how Martin conjured up a meal in such a confined space; I would need more space to make a sandwich, let alone a meal. Whenever we wild camp, Dave cooks yards away from the tent and has his little kitchen placed on a few rocks, fearing the stove could tip. You may have gathered that we don't intentionally camp in a howling gale or pouring rain. On the odd occasion we've been caught out, it's been a sandwich and a cold drink inside the tent. It's hardly a life-and-death situation doing without hot refreshment. Whenever we visited Scotland, three nights had been the agreed time limit for roughing it. How things change.

Martin perched himself inside the tent beside the porch. Adjacent to his tiny stove were a few bags containing a variety of packets: freeze-dried meals, noodles, tins of tuna, pasta, soup, mash, cous-cous (my least favourite), and even custard and the odd pudding. Savoury biscuits with cheese triangles were handed around, along with the weapon of mass destruction aka salami. Much as we might have liked a slice, that wasn't feasible. A slab that size at that altitude had become a rock, frozen solid and impossible to cut without a chainsaw.

When it came to provisions to eat on the hoof, Martin dished out nuts, raisins, cereal bars, cheese and chocolate. We were five little hamsters complete with pantries stuffed in their mouths, cheeks bulging as they walked. Removing wrappers before setting off made eating on the move more efficient. Even I realised that the route would not be classified as a 'picnic mountain'!

Martin used a walkie-talkie to contact Naveen at base camp for weather reports when he could get a signal, though it seemed somewhat erratic. If the weather played ball, we would move to summit camp the following day. The orange tent was dismantled in preparation, one less chore for the morning, and Dawa moved in with us.

Did Dawa realise he had drawn the short straw? You'd be correct in thinking I was developing a complex. Thank goodness he wasn't the porter who carried the machete – there could have been a massacre if there was a disagreement, and Dave and I would have been easy pickings as we were in the same tent!

Monday 8th October – Advance Base Camp – Snowbound

MORE SNOW HAD fallen overnight and the plan to head to summit camp went the same way as many other plans. As we were snowbound, most of us would be having a day off – but for Dave, Martin and Dawa it was anything but a holiday. The three of them would carry as much gear and food as possible, climb onto the glacier and hopefully find a suitable spot for summit camp.

One observation that struck me about the Himalaya was the prolonged process to achieve height and distance due to the altitude and the conditions. It was a case of up and down, retracing your steps, slowly edging your way to the climax of the trip. I remember thinking that if it took much longer, I'd forget where I was heading! I was eager to get to the nitty-gritty; I'm an impatient soul when it comes to most things in life.

Dawa came to me and asked for some gloves. He'd misplaced a pair that Martin had given him, so maybe I seemed the better option to ask for replacements. I had two pairs of gloves in total; I would have preferred more back-ups, but we had to keep things to a minimum. Hand on my heart, I can say that my main pair of mountaineering gloves were more substantial but too small for Dawa. The reserve pair had more stretch and were still very warm so that's what I gave him. I can now say my Marks and Spencer £8.50 Thinsulate gloves have been to a height of over 5000m (16400+ft). Possibly an advert in the offing M&S? I'm sure we can come to an agreement!

The three men left camp at around 6.30am. I had a couple more hours of sleep and then I was awake, home alone in the tent. I listened to a little music then went outside to sit and make notes. The fabric of the blue tent seemed quite dense and let in little light, giving a rather oppressive and far from cosy feel. I was keeping the use of my headtorch to an absolute minimum as it was becoming ever-more unreliable. It had become a mini-lighthouse, flashing on and off. I decided to change the battery when we reached summit camp.

Time was difficult to judge in those conditions but after maybe an hour I retreated to my tent. Altitude and lack of sleep seemed to have affected Lynne's personality but now it was my turn for emotional issues. The sleeping problem was festering as I mulled it over. Those who know me well are fully aware that I take the silliest of things to heart and my concerns can last for months.

Anita, Carl and Lynne were still in their tent and I was convinced I had been sent to Coventry when I hadn't been invited to join them. They knew I was on my own. Was this my punishment for getting up too many times in the night? As the minutes ticked by, the blacker my mood became. It never entered my head that they might be asleep; that was far too logical an explanation! There were three people only a stone's throw away and yet I felt so lonely. There have been plenty of times when I have been on my own and never felt that way.

I went outside again, hoping that the mountains would offer reassurance. They didn't; they had also deserted me and offered no comfort whatsoever. Instead, a little black dog called 'self-doubt', along with his mates 'insecurity and anxiety', nipped at my heels. I had never known them venture into the mountains before.

Then I heard a voice call out from the yellow tent, 'Sue, why don't you join us?'

We listened to music and chatted. Anita and Lynne were cocooned in their sleeping bags and wearing their down jackets. I had my jacket on but I would have melted had I been in a sleeping bag. Carl was not looking well and, even when we decided to stretch our legs and have a cuppa, he was reluctant to move. That was totally out of character.

The clouds vanished and for a while we sat outside drinking tea in the sunshine, wondering how the other three were coping. Then the clouds returned bringing snow, so we retreated into the yellow tent for even more sorting of rucksacks.

I wasn't happy if I was without my hand gel or worrying about sleeping arrangements, and Lynne was only content if she was rearranging her rucksack. The more she rearranged, the more harassed she became. I think altitude has a lot to answer for!

Anita was a dab hand at managing all manner of tasks within the confines of her sleeping bag and Carl seemed satisfied with all female company ... he was definitely ailing!

Time was getting on; it was no good, I had to go outside and wait for the menfolk to return. Visibility was poor but I managed to discern a figure in the distance. Who it was I couldn't tell, but there was only one.

The solitary figure was Dawa, covered in blood. My heart missed a beat as a sickly feeling welled up inside me – then I saw that Dawa was having a nose bleed. 'What's happened, where are the others?' I asked. There was no answer to my question.

I ran to my tent to find something for the nose bleed – and promptly fell over a boulder. Two golden rules of first aid: do not rush, and look out for potential dangers. I'd broken both rules in a matter of seconds. It's most unlike me to rush, and medicine fascinates me: blood and guts have never been a problem (though you're on your own when it comes to poo and puke). A nose bleed was hardly life-threatening so there was no particular urgency, but I was desperate for an answer to my question.

I hit the boulder with considerable force, my shin taking the brunt of the impact. It was agony but I screamed silently. Dawa still required attention so I hobbled to the yellow tent in search of help. I left him in their capable hands and got the gist that Dave and Martin were following behind.

I couldn't wait any longer. I started to retrace Dawa's footsteps but fortunately, within a matter of moments, the missing persons appeared, seemingly in one piece. The pain returned to my shin, which was now bleeding.

I was so lucky to escape with a minor injury. I have never regarded myself as accident prone, but I do seem to be unlucky. In the few years I worked at the bank, I once fell off my stool and caught an alarm button. Half the Bradford police constabulary descended on the branch, to be told that some foolish teenage cashier had fallen. First names were never used by management when addressing junior staff: 'Miss Stones, my office now!'

By the looks on their faces and their general demeanour, it was obvious that the day had been anything but easy; however, they had found a suitable spot for summit camp. Deep snow had hampered their progress but it was the minefield of crevasses that had been difficult and dangerous in one section. One crevasse seemed to cut the glacier in two with no obvious way around. There looked to be a feasible snow-bridge; the only snag was its location eight feet down inside the crevasse. Roped up, they had climbed down one by one to the bridge; it held, and then they climbed back out on the other side. It was deemed too risky to use on the return journey.

The boss found a diversion in the shape of a boulder-strewn gully running along the edge of the glacier, not ideal but less hazardous. They had also placed markers made of twigs and red ribbon to aid navigation through the unavoidable crevasses in readiness for our ascent.

I was so proud of Dave; it seemed he had become Sherpa Pugh. Thankfully I only heard about this at a much later stage. I can't begin to imagine how severe the expeditions are that Martin offers in the 'most difficult' category. The ratings start at A and go up to D; our expedition was bespoke so it had no grade but I think we were still in the shallow end. Although Martin hadn't visited Sikkim before, he had gleaned some knowledge from a friend who had climbed Brumkhangse eleven years previously. I am sure the face of the glacier had have changed considerably in that space of time, but any information was useful.

I was more upbeat once I knew that everyone was safe, but the disturbed sleep business hadn't totally vanished and I felt sure at some stage we would be sharing a tent again. I had a quiet word with Dave. He often struggles to understand my train of thought, but he remained calm and offered his logical words of wisdom. How many times had people happily shared our tent in Scotland? Had anyone declined the offer? Our night-time trips to the loo were hardly a secret and they hadn't prevented anybody sharing with us. So, what was the difference? None.

I mooted the idea of drinking less but Dave pointed out that hydration was important. After suggesting another idea, that we combined our pee visits, I realised I was pushing Dave's patience. 'Sue, our habits haven't changed. Carry on as we do in Scotland!' he said.

I realised it would be prudent for me to drop the subject; message received and understood.

Tuesday 9th October – Advance Base Camp – Summit Camp

AT LAST, SUNSHINE. Dawa had been in our tent for a second night but today he was returning to his longed-for base camp after first accompanying us to the snout of the glacier. There was more equipment to transport and then it would be down to us to lug it up the last section.

I now had more of a feel for a nomadic lifestyle. I am a home-bird and find comfort from security, but I accepted packing and unpacking comparatively well. With items scattered about the mountain at summit camp and at the hidey-hole, there was less to pack at advance base camp. There was also less to consider about what required packing because nothing could be abandoned. By now carrying all and sundry was perfectly acceptable; de- sensitisation seems to have great powers.

The black clouds, which had been knocking hell out of my emotions the previous day, had vanished. I was upbeat about what lay ahead, proof if any was needed that ignorance can be bliss. At last, I could look forward to seeing my goal, Brumkhangse.

I remembered a walk with Anita and Lynne in the Yorkshire Dales when we finished at a pub in Burnsall. Just for a change, our conversation revolved around the Himalaya trip. It soon became apparent we had different goals; I seemed to be the only one who's main focus was to climb Brumkhangse. Summiting the mountain appeared to be incidental to Anita and Lynne – great if it happened but more of an optional extra. I know Dave and I were in agreement; if a peak hadn't been included from the outset, Dave most certainly would not have been interested. As for Carl, I don't know his thoughts on the matter; perhaps his priority was bagging Munros!

We were walking by 7am. I doubt we'd been going more than an hour when it was decided that Carl could not, and should not, go any further. For the first half hour we lost a little height but he struggled for breath as soon as we arrived at the slightest incline; his face was swollen and he was dragging rather than lifting his leg. He opted to stay where he was and wait until Dawa returned. They could go down together.

Martin impressed on Carl that if he felt no better at base camp, he must instruct Naveen to arrange transport to take him lower still to Lachung. This was an advantage of the revised itinerary that included the use of vehicles: we could reach lower altitudes more quickly in the event of such a problem.

They say altitude sickness can strike anybody and there appears to be no logic behind it. People who have never suffered for years can suddenly be struck down; health and fitness seem to be immaterial. It was a blow to leave Carl but a reminder, if we needed one, of the seriousness of where we were.

We pressed on to the hidey-hole to collect the gear that had been left and to leave other items. This was a kit inspection with a difference: it wasn't merely a case of ensuring we had everything we required but rather the opposite. Anything that wasn't absolutely essential must be left behind. Keeping weight to a minimum could make all the difference.

We emptied our rucksacks and the boss inspected the contents of various bags. I was deemed to be carrying too many tops. I know I don't feel the cold but… I did as I was told. We were instructed to leave our crampon bags behind – unnecessary baggage. Dave was not asked to remove anything but given extra items to carry as we would no longer have a porter after we said goodbye to Dawa.

The grading of the route, together with the adrenaline, went up a notch as we prepared for the glacier. We donned harnesses and crampons, then we roped-up with Martin in the lead, the women in the middle and Dave bringing up the rear.

Our welcoming committee was in the shape of a steep snowbank to gain access to the glacier. Martin kicked steps into the top layer of soft snow. Even when the steps were there, I still found it tough when the imprints gave way under pressure. With less oxygen, it was knackering. Yes, a bad workman blames her tools, and in this case it was my legs!

I was praying for cloud cover because, although we were wearing sunhats, the heat from the sun reflecting off the snow was absurdly hot. I felt like a fried egg on legs as my internal thermometer went into orbit, while Anita and Lynne lapped up the warmth.

Once on the glacier it seemed a little easier, though Martin still had to weave his way through the crevasses. The footsteps from the previous day had been obliterated by fresh snow. We followed, concentrating on keeping the correct distance apart and the correct tension on the rope. If anybody fell into a hidden crevasse, the next person should be far enough away not to end up in the crevasse themselves. By the same token, if the tension was correct the rope wouldn't snatch; excessive force could pull a person over.

Our next objective was the gully that the men had used on their return. I had a happy knack of finding all the hidden holes lurking beneath the soft snow, invariably filled with water, which hindered my progress as my crampons jammed in the confined spaces. It was only then that it dawned on me that I had forgotten all about my less-than-desirable B2¾ boots. Finally, we were friends!

We exited the gully and headed in the direction of summit camp. What a relief to arrive at our new abode. The women were shattered but goodness knows how the men felt when this was their second visit within a matter of hours. The small orange tent was already in place, courtesy of the men the previous day; now the large yellow tent required assembling. Everyone was desperate for a hot drink but drinking was a luxury that would have to wait until our home was ready.

Afternoon cloud drew a veil over the sun just when the sun might have been welcome. I felt no fear, but taking in my whereabouts brought it home: this was one serious, unforgiving environment and not a place for the faint hearted. Our lives were in Martin's hands, though the unpredictably of the mountains is out of everybody's hands.

Anita and Lynne would have the delights of the Pughs in their tent. I worried far less about their opinions; having crevasses for neighbours and altitude at 5135m (16847 ft) seemed to redirect my thoughts.

There was no need for our own entertainment that evening; nature provided us with a top-class display. There was a backdrop of twinkling stars wherever you looked, the Milky Way, shooting stars and the mountains silhouetted against the snow. Absolutely stunning. One more precious reward for our labours. I'd wondered what would it be like, up there away from humanity, but even my rainbows didn't stretch that far!

The idea that our new headtorches would light up the night sky couldn't have been further from the truth. Lynne's had totally given up the ghost and, although I changed the batteries, mine had developed a mind of its own.

Eating a hot meal seemed an effort and a drink would have sufficed as far as I was concerned. This was a much lengthier process compared to our previous 'homes' where there had been running water, not quite on tap but close enough. Now it was a case of shovelling snow, which then needed to be melted and heated. Every aspect of living became a task.

Wednesday 10th October – Summit Camp – Col – Summit Camp

WE LEFT OUR boots inside the tent porch overnight but by the following morning they were rock solid, with the laces frozen just as we had left them. Dave's and mine were slightly less solid as they'd been worn during the night on our nocturnal wanderings. Martin put his boots inside his sleeping bag; I knew to keep clothes inside my sleeping bag but not boots – surely they would wet the bag? The expedition virgins were learning something new every day.

It was another sunny morning with even more amazing views, except for one view that was slightly less amazing… Martin commented he was tired of seeing Dave's buttocks popping up from behind a boulder. Dave considered his bowels to be fine but the times he visited the boulder indicated the contrary. I passed him a dose of Imodium which, to my surprise, he took without question.

Then he admitted he'd forgotten his toilet roll and was relying on an emergency pack he kept in his rucksack. Share and share alike, but I rationed it to so many pieces at a time. I'm not too sure what Dave does with the stuff. We know most of one another's intimate habits but thankfully the ins and outs of his loo-paper use remain a mystery. The quantity he goes through is nobody's business; anybody would think he's about to wallpaper a room.

Ingenuity was required. What did we have? An abundance

of snow. We would share my precious roll, but first we'd use a snowball, lightly scuffed at the edges. It worked but it was bloody cold! A smooth finish on the snowball was about as much use as that old-fashioned toilet paper from donkey's years ago that came with a shiny side. Who on earth invented that!

At one stage I couldn't help but laugh at the whole toilet affair. Nature called; I lost my balance and ended up standing in the deposit. I could either laugh or cry at this utter madness. A boot in need of urgent cleaning, a frozen bum from the snowball treatment, and a headtorch that was busy sending out Morse code as it flashed on and off. This is the person who wouldn't book a hotel room without en-suite facilities and who vowed never to camp, let alone wild camp. Giggling uncontrollably with another snowball in my hand as I cleaned my boot, I whispered to myself, 'Sue, what *are* you doing here!' But standards hadn't completely been abandoned as I could still spray myself with Eternity.

We found another use for the snow: it worked well for washing up the pans and mugs. The washing-up snow was sourced well away from the toilet-snowball zone.

Fed and watered, we went on another reconnoitre, aiming to gain height and reach the col at 5370m (17618 ft). At the same time, we could make clear tracks in readiness for summit day if it didn't snow again.

We snaked our way through more crevasses and utilised the gully at the side. Poor Anita had been feeling less than well. Gut issues: she described it as 'feeling like a washing machine churning and gurgling'. She came to a halt and announced she couldn't go any further. We left her in a comparatively safe spot; we would be returning the same way to collect her.

Finally we saw our goal, Brumkhangse, bigger than I had imagined and steeper than I'd expected. I felt sure its steepness was a trick of the light and the angle we were at; after all, this was a trekking peak. There's always a steady way up – it was simply hidden from view. Stop laughing, all you experts out there!

We turned round at the col and headed back to collect Anita. Safely back at summit camp, and before the predictable mid-afternoon cloud, we looked forward to a coffee. A pile of snow went into the Jet Boil (other makes are available). There was the usual ritual of waiting for the snow to melt and the water to boil before we got the end product in our mugs, but it passed the time of day. The thought of making a drink at the flick of a switch in the 'civilised' world seemed mundane and uninteresting.

It was good to be huddled together enjoying a relaxed atmosphere with Anita feeling a little better. Tomorrow would be the big day. I was so pleased I hadn't suffered from gut issues and I seemed to be coping well with the altitude. In fact, other than Martin, I think I was the healthiest of us all. Miracles will never cease.

Enough of the chit-chat, Martin wanted our attention. 'Okay, folks, we have a suitable weather window tomorrow to attempt the summit. I shall be taking Dave and Lynne with me.'

You could have heard a pin drop. Don't ask why, but I travelled back in time to my schooldays and raised my hand as you would to attract the teacher's attention. I fell short of saying 'Please, sir' but politely said, 'But I would like to come.' Martin had clearly forgotten to call my name.

He continued and I thought I heard the words 'I'm sorry, Sue', but perhaps it was 'Sue, I'm sorry.' The good weather window was small before conditions would deteriorate. It was imperative to be back at summit camp ahead of the weather and Martin felt I would be too slow. He suspected that the final push could entail technical sections that I'd struggle with. If we were caught out, it would be dangerous. That was a word I hardly ever heard Martin use.

The silence was deafening. There was no more fooling myself, I wasn't going. Nobody said a word as I frantically fought back the tears as my world crumbled with every breath I took. I looked at Dave in disbelief but he was unable to utter a word as tears welled up in his eyes.

Anita and Lynne remained silent until Lynne whispered, 'But we're a team.'

Under normal circumstances, I would question information that I found unpalatable but that never entered my head. I'm so pleased I held onto my dignity, albeit by the skin of my teeth; at least I was crying silently and not blubbing.

Dave finally looked at me and said he couldn't go without me.

'Yes, you can,' I replied.

Martin suggested one other option. If I went with them, it would be on the basis that if we fell behind schedule we'd abort the attempt on the summit and everyone would retreat. It was a no-brainer: I could not take the risk of being responsible for ruining the others' chances of summiting.

I felt physically sick. I wanted to be anywhere other than where I was, but that was not possible so it was time to get a grip. Ever since we'd left Hellifield, I had tucked my flag inside my rucksack for fear I would forget it at the vital moment. Just like those rainbows, the picture I'd been carrying in my head for nearly fifteen months vanished into thin air; it was time to handover the baton. A quick rummage and I placed the flag firmly in Dave's hand. 'Just you make sure you fly that flag up there.'

I'm sure we had a meal together, and I'm sure there was conversation, but neither registered. I was no longer there – yet sadly I was. Lynne seemed laden with guilt because she had been chosen but I felt no malice towards her. She is a natural climber and I'm not; her technical skills are far better than mine and therefore she is faster.

Martin instructed us that the alarm should be set for midnight for the explorers to depart at 1.30am. With an unearthly hour, temperatures well below zero, pitch blackness and a wonky headtorch, it did cross my mind there were some hidden benefits when you're the runt of the pack. I could remain snug in my sleeping bag.

Anita was also out of the equation for summiting because of her health issues. Martin had grave reservations about leaving her on her own, and the absence of a high-altitude porter compounded matters. So, in the face of adversity, I came in handy in some small way. But I felt that Anita's illness, rather like Carl's, was a more acceptable reason for missing out on the summit attempt.

Dave and Lynne were busy packing their rucksacks. Most of the gear could be packed but one or two items might be required overnight and were put aside. Lynne questioned whether she was capable of what lay ahead and if it was the correct thing to do morally, as this expedition had been my idea. I insisted there should be no guilt and Martin would not have chosen her if he'd had any doubts about her ability. I could speak from first-hand experience!

Since the visit to the Himalaya, I have concluded that gathering gear and packing should be practised within the confines of a broom cupboard. It's all well and good when there is ample space to spread out everything, but when there are four people in a tent together with their belongings, a lot of which bear a strong resemblance to your own, it's a nightmare of a task. The only alternative is to drag everything outside and pack in sub-zero temperatures. That can be preferable to a crowded tent in daylight but, once darkness falls and you only have two working headtorches between five people, the broom cupboard gets the vote.

It was time to get some sleep. As you know, I'm one of those lucky people who rarely have problems sleeping but that night was different. It felt rather like a bereavement: the shock and numbness, followed by tears and emptiness, at the same time analysing everything. I wondered if, or when, anger would rear its ugly head and when true acceptance of the situation would make an appearance.

I was unprepared for the situation I found myself in. It had never entered my head. We'd talked often about illness, altitude and bad weather putting a stop to summiting, but never considered that our skills or speed could be inadequate. What would I say to people when I got home? Questions and answers were buzzing in my head. There was only one thing I could say and that was the truth: I wasn't good enough.

Would I have stood a better chance on a well-known mountain that Martin had climbed before? Should I have attended the gym more often – although I'm not too sure how that would have improved my skills. It was futile kicking these ifs and buts around in my head because I couldn't turn back the clock. This was the face of serious winter mountaineering, where rewards could be immense but any show of weakness had serious consequences. You play by very different rules, whether they are hard to swallow or not.

My next train of thought was that I'd wasted my time and money; I should have booked a 'manicured-tourist' trek and become one of the many ants following one group after another. Deep down, I knew I didn't think that at all.

I'm sure you get the picture as I argued with myself but I did not begrudge Dave and Lynne.

Thursday 11th October – Summit Day

SLEEP IS A good anaesthetic but it was disturbed by the sound of the alarm pinging in the background. Back to reality. I hadn't been having nightmares; sadly I was still in the same place, in the middle of nowhere with the same thoughts, although at that very moment I did not envy the others. I could observe from the comfort of my 'bed', and the first glimmer of humour entered my head. I came under the same classification as the crampon bags, abandoned in the hidey-hole – unnecessary baggage that would slow down the group!

For a good twenty minutes, Lynne was in search of her over-trousers which had gone walkabout in the tent. A black garment in a poorly-lit tent, where most objects appeared to be black, was not helping matters. Martin was showing concern; it was well past departure time. He made a few suggestions: was Lynne already wearing them, or could she borrow mine? Unfortunately, I couldn't help. I was wearing mountaineering trousers which didn't require over-trousers; if I handed over my trousers that would leave me with my long johns (aka passion killers) for the next few hours. Although I withstand the cold extremely well, even I would be pushing my luck on that one! Lynne also had mountaineering trousers but required the over-trousers as an extra layer for warmth.

Martin's next idea was to use Anita's trousers. We pointed out the difference in leg length: Lynne is petite, Anita is tall. 'You have no choice, you will have to stuff them down your

Martin on the snout of the glacier

Summit Camp

Utilising a boulder-strewn gully to avoid crevasses

Weather rolling in at Summit Camp

Brumkhangse summit & Yorkshire flag unfurled,
with a jaw dropping vista behind

Martin on the final approach to Brumkhangse summit

Martin and prayer flags on the summit of Brumkhangse

gaiters,' came the reply.

Laurel and Hardy would have been proud of the spectacle that was unravelling had it not been a serious situation. By 2am Anita and I were left in peace after Martin handed over the walkie-talkie. A few minutes later, I wondered if I would know what to do should an emergency arise. I was sure Anita and I could fathom it out if push came to shove. I half-wondered if it was a placebo, but why worry? I really didn't care.

I fell asleep again immediately, which was useful in more ways than one. The only working headtorches had been taken by the intrepid three, since their need was far greater. And we thought we would be lighting up the skies… It was a lesson in caution when everybody buys the same gear. It seemed that the torches were averse to altitude. Dave was right: I should have stuck with my old faithful Petzl. His was working a treat. Another lesson: carry a spare headtorch rather than spare batteries; there's not that much difference in weight.

As a standby, I was using the torch on my phone but only if absolutely necessary. To think I frowned upon people having a love affair with their phones. Mine had become a vital piece of equipment.

It appeared bright outside through the yellow fabric of our house. Unzipping the tent revealed a beautiful day. I had no idea what time it was but it did not matter. The first job was to go for a pee once I could lay my hands on my sunglasses; that certainly wasn't a case of posing but rather a practicality to prevent snow blindness. With brilliant sunshine illuminating the snow, it was virtually impossible to see without protection.

Sorted; now for a cuppa. I was pleasantly surprised that I managed to light the stove. I'd practised the day before using the fire starter/flint. This was another example of something I'd previously left to Dave. Without a spark we wouldn't be having a drink, so it was a good incentive to try! We chose to sit outside, sipping our tea, wondering how the early birds were coping.

Anita suggested we could spring-clean the tents. I believe this is how she is at home: never stopping and always looking for the next task. I tend to wonder if something really needs my attention and I would rather be doing something else. However, on this occasion I agreed; it would be useful to give the sleeping bags, sleep mats and anything else that was damp and smelly an airing.

Eureka! Lynne's over-trousers made a guest appearance having somehow spent the night hiding under Dave's sleep mat. Obviously, they didn't fancy the summit. With articles of clothing being thrown about the place, it was hardly surprising they were lost. I suspect that, considering the turmoil Lynne was in, she might have also chosen to go into hiding.

It was surprising how time slipped by doing this and that, collecting more snow for the stove and for washing up. With the tents encircled by crevasses, we'd been given strict instructions not to stray far. It was Anita's turn to have a meander, so I plonked myself down on a boulder.

I looked around and saw nothing. For long enough I avoided eye contact with Brumkhangse, but slowly I began to simmer and quickly came to the boil. Enough was enough. I turned and glared at my nemesis. 'Fuck you,' I shouted and I began to cry. For a few moments I hated everything, everyone, but most of all I hated myself. I can vouch that jealousy is a dangerous emotion that only succeeds in screwing you up. I glanced upward, watching a fluffy cottonwool cloud drifting by. Oh, to be that cloud and fly away. That was the only way I would reach the summit.

I remembered a remark that somebody made when I first booked the expedition: 'The experience and walk in will be as much a pleasure as the peak.' Wearing my rarely-used logical head, I evaluated my situation. It was time for a kick up the backside; stop this 'woe is me' and accept reality. The glass was half-full, not half-empty. Few people were lucky enough to be where I was.

Open your eyes, Sue, look around you. Pleasure was in abundance. The views: hundreds of peaks highlighted with snow against a backdrop of blue that stretched as far as the eye could see, with not a trace of civilisation. The peace, tranquillity and exquisite beauty of this untamed wilderness was breathtaking. I don't know about searching for rainbows, I was cloaked in one and could not see it!

A few words plucked me from the edge of a black hole I was teetering on. Ever since we'd booked the trip, I had glossed over one simple word that featured in Martin's correspondence: 'attempt'. *Attempt* the summit. Now it was beginning to make sense.

It's the same principal for any mountain. We had been turned back several times in the Highlands due to weather. This was on a much larger scale but here the reason was more complex, which made it hard to accept. That's what comes from playing in the big-boys' league. Would I have preferred a trek or a peak with more certainty of success? Most definitely not. And after all, what is success? Moran Mountain have a code of ethics which can be found on their website and it's well worth a read. Summiting is not the be all and end all.

By mid-afternoon the sky had turned a murky grey and the fluffy white clouds had been replaced with their rather more menacing relatives as visibility deteriorated dramatically. Anita and I were back in the relative safety of the tent. I was becoming anxious and kept popping my head out until eventually I thought I saw figures appearing out of the gloom. On with the boots and everything except the now-redundant sunglasses.

It all seemed to be happening in slow motion. I could see them, but their progress seemed painfully slow. I did a headcount: all present and correct so I would have to be patient. I wish I could say I ran to meet them but I would be telling porkies. Run? Certainly not at that altitude!

I couldn't greet them simultaneously so it had to be Dave. I was all smiles and giddy but I was alone in that. The first words Dave uttered were, 'Thank Martin. He's done you a favour. You would have hated it. You couldn't have managed that.'

There was no sign of excitement or elation, just relief. I was beginning to think they hadn't summited but they had reached their goal. I glanced across at Lynne to see a blank, expressionless face. Anita was close by; she grabbed Lynne, gave her a big hug and took her into the tent where Lynne cried uncontrollably. My God, what on earth had happened?

Martin returned to his tent. Perhaps he felt this was our special time together but also it was a time for him to relive his own adventure. He may be a mountain guide but that doesn't exclude him from emotions and passion for the mountains. I've just realised that nobody greeted the boss on his return ... sorry, Martin!

After a hot drink and a bite to eat, Dave and Lynne started to share their experiences with us. Lynne's headtorch had packed in before they left, as had mine, so she had borrowed Anita's which showed a tiny glimmer of life. Within ten minutes of departure that also died so Lynne was reliant on the beam of Dave's torch behind her to light her way. This procedure works to a certain extent, but if the person behind so much as glances to one side or another the person in front is plunged into darkness – less than ideal in a boulder-strewn gully.

Dave half-hoped that dawn would break by the time they reached the col but it didn't. After a quick break, the serious climbing began. As Martin went ahead, Dave and Lynne marvelled on how he managed in the dark, albeit with a working headtorch. He found every twist and turn on a route he had never climbed before and with nothing to follow. They were observing a professional at work with years of experience under his belt.

It was steep, ice and snow with an ever-changing consistency: hard then soft; soft layered on hard, and then the delights of a knife-edge arête. Large accumulations of snow had transformed a steep-angled side into a vertical wall of snow, which necessitated stepping over the knife edge to the other side. Mission accomplished until the next obstacle reared its head, this time in the form of an outcrop of rock covered in ice and blocking the line of attack.

The line of least resistance was left of centre on the outcrop. Lynne doubted she could make the manoeuvre over to the left but, with Dave behind her offering a helping hand, she managed. The outcrop was ticked off – and yet another precipitous arête awaited their attention.

They used a variety of gizmos along the way: ice screws; huge aluminium spikes that were hammered into the ice to set up belays: slings and krabs (remember those?), to name but a few. The summit was within reach and now the ground was at an easier angle but there were still crevasses to avoid.

Victory, as the flag was unfurled at the summit. Dawa had asked Martin to take some prayer-flags to fly. All three were over the moon at their triumph and, with the benefit of daylight, they were rewarded with jaw-dropping views. On this rare occasion the word awesome was worthy. Hopefully the photograph will give you a flavour.

It was wonderful to be on top but there was the small matter of the return journey. Most of the route would be down-climbed, in other words facing into the mountain and going down backwards. The few sections that they could attempt facing outwards would still be difficult. Lynne did not welcome the thought – I wonder why?! I would have found the idea of slitting my throat more acceptable.

On the return leg they had a bird's-eye view of the rash of crevasses that peppered the landscape, showing their footsteps weaving in and out of the minefield. The blank expressions and words that they uttered on their return now made perfect sense; it was shell-shock and fatigue. But what an amazing achievement and I, for one, was genuinely proud and happy for them. Hell's teeth – I'd just been saved from a fate worse than death.

Was this a typical trekking peak? No, it wasn't. According to Martin, it would require fixed ropes and ladders before it could be regarded as such. Hearing this gave me renewed hope that there might be a mountain out there I could manage, but I still would not choose one that all and sundry often climb. There's no pleasing some folk; I always want the impossible, or what seems impossible.

Apparently, the term 'trekking peak' can be slightly mis-leading. The price for a permit to climb a mountain is dependent on the category of the mountain. Brumkhangse was in the trekking-peak price bracket, but not a typical trekking peak. I realise my description is clear as mud, so please forgive me, but it's reminiscent of the easiest route onto Sgur nan Gillean on Skye. It's called the tourist route and to a climber would be a stroll in the park, but to an average walker (and most certainly a 'tourist') that couldn't be further from the truth.

Lynne's fuel tank was on empty but it was surprising how quickly food and rest gave her a boost. Both she and Dave were so pleased at their success, and rightly so. Lynne vowed she would never attempt anything as difficult ever again; we'll see! It would be many weeks later before she allowed herself a well-deserved pat on the back.

Her elation was marred by the guilt she felt. It was *my* trip, *my* idea, and three of us were missing. The event had been tinged with sadness because of the unforeseen situation but that was down to our naivety. The more you learn, the more you realise how very little you know.

Food stocks were low and our evening 'meal' consisted of fruitcake and custard.

Summit   5635metres   18,487 feet

Col 5370 metres   17,618 feet

Summit Camp 5135 metres   16, 847 feet

Glacier Snout/'Hidey-Hole'
4675 metres   15,337 feet

Advance Base Camp   4540 metres   14,895 feet

Drop-off Point/Dumping Area
4400 metres 14,435 feet

Base Camp   3915 metres   12,844 feet

Friday 12th October – Summit Camp – Base Camp – Lachung

I WAS VAGUELY aware of a slight headache during the night but I was also aware the tent sides were flapping. It sounded a little windy but I drifted back into the Land of Nod. It was the first time there'd been any wind, a noticeable difference to Scotland particularly taking into account the altitude.

Daylight revealed an unwelcome sight. A lot of snow had fallen and the tents were sagging; there was low cloud, an odd snow flurry and appalling visibility. Packing up in those conditions required a determined approach. Our surroundings were far from inviting and the mountains made it abundantly clear that we'd overstayed our welcome.

We were returning to base camp but I had no idea how on earth Martin would suss a route out through the crevasses, some of which were now hidden. There had been little room for error when we could see them. However, our immediate concern was the amount of equipment that we needed to carry back down. There were no porters, just us until we were off the glacier. Theoretically there would be helping hands at the snout of the glacier but this was by no means a certainty, and first we needed to get there.

The only item left behind was the salami. I was given the honour of launching the missile in the general direction of the nearest crevasse. I hoped Mr Yeti wasn't down there taking a nap; the poor lad would have been knocked senseless if that had landed on his head. Perhaps in many years to come, as glaciers melt and divulge their contents, the salami might make a guest appearance.

Our rucksacks were bulging and we took it in turn to help each other lift them onto our back. They were far too heavy to lift in the usual way and none of us had carried such weights before. Without a porter, Dave and Martin were carrying well in excess of twenty kilos each. They are both fit but age has to be a consideration: sixty-nine and sixty-three years old respectively does not do load-carrying abilities any favours.

We used trekking poles to aid stability and once more we roped up. There was no talking; each of us was watching every step we took. Standing on a snow-bridge only the width of a plank, looking down into a yawning chasm, acted as a huge reminder of the danger.

We paused. I tied my boots a little tighter and Martin surveyed the situation. He was far from happy because we weren't where he wanted to be. Anita noted one of the markers they'd deposited a few days earlier was over to the left. Had there not been crevasses, it would have been a simple case of altering course.

There we were, a band of old-age pensioners on our first Himalaya experience, in the midst of a maze of crevasses with zero visibility. This would have been serious with a group of seasoned mountaineers but our inexperience of the Himalaya probably exacerbated Martin's worries. He chose a different line of attack: continue slightly to the right and ultimately swing left below the crevasses but at a more acute angle. I sensed this was very much a case of 'the devil and the deep', a situation Martin did not relish. Now we would be blindfold on unchartered terrain.

No sooner had Martin solved one problem than another took its place. Momentarily I lost my footing, something or nothing in the normal run of things, but my fully-laden rucksack accentuated the movement and tipped me off balance. I was now on my bum, slithering off to the right though not too far as I was roped up. The next second Anita decided to keep me company. Dave, the anchor man, did a brilliant job and the brakes went on, which prevented Lynne slipping. There I was, on my back, doing a good impression of a turtle upside down with its legs in the air.

The boss man shouted orders:

1. *Roll onto my front and kick a ledge to stand on, using the points on my crampons.* Rolling over was easier said than done with the size of my rucksack but I obeyed. Kicking a ledge came easier.

2. *Take my rucksack off and get out my ice axe.* Tricky, but I managed.

3. *Put rucksack back on.* Bloody difficult considering the weight, but I ticked the box.

4. *Dagger ice axe into snow and climb back up ....* mission accomplished.

The skills I had learned over the years were used in anger for the first time. This was no training slope; there was no local mountain rescue and no helicopter to hand. We were five people alone in the world, just surviving.

Anita had similar instructions but when it came to getting her rucksack back on her energy was totally spent, I suspect as the result of her gut problems. Lynne placed her axe in position to act as anchor for Dave, who climbed down to help Anita. Martin could not come to our aid, hence the instructions from a distance: he was the anchor at the front ensuring our safety.

In the middle of this nightmare scenario, Martin shouted out, clinging to the possibility that the porters might be waiting for us at the snout of the glacier. Three days had elapsed without radio contact, so Martin had no idea if anybody would be there to meet us.

Voices pierced the void: either the angels were summoning us or it could be the porters.

It wasn't much further before we arrived at the snowbank we'd climbed a couple of days earlier. Martin belayed us as we down-climbed: Dave, Lynne, Anita and then me. Everybody was steady away except me. I started rather cautiously until I was instructed to go a little faster. Martin was in control of the belay so however much rope he let out was as far as I could go. I was given plenty of rope so, sod it, I would do a mini abseil.

The others couldn't believe it when I caught them up. I think I had been given plenty of 'slack' because, with much relief, Martin could see our porters waiting to catch us. It was the fastest I'd moved in days!

We'd survived the glacial experience and finally the porters could take most of the heavy gear. Nevertheless, we still had the items in the hidey-hole to retrieve and a lengthy walk to base camp through wet slushy snow. We spent another five exhausting hours staggering down this endless mountainside, with only the benefit of a few biscuits eaten earlier that morning.

De-sensitisation was again my saviour: one foot in front of the other, interspersed with the odd falter. My mind had drawn a veil over thirst, hunger, fatigue or pain. Had we been forced to carry everything ourselves, the outcome did not bear thinking about.

We were encouraged to up our speed in order to reach base camp in time for our meal before packing up and driving down to Lachung. There was a lot to fit in the time available. I wonder if Martin has ever told somebody to slow down. None of us have heard those words!

It seemed the whole village had turned out to welcome us back, waving and on the verge of cheering. Binodh had enquired about weather forecasts at the nearby military post and been told that they did not envy anyone up in the mountains. We learned at a later stage that, sadly, nine climbers were killed that day in Nepal when the weather caught them out.

Not only were we treated like heroes but we also received white scarves. I tried to explain that I hadn't summited. I felt I didn't deserve a gift with guilt hanging over my head, but they insisted I should have a scarf.

It was lovely to be reunited with Carl and heaven to eat a hot meal. Egg and chips, the best egg and chips I've ever tasted. It was only then that Martin confessed my Song of Sikkim, 'Think Twice', had been ringing in his ears on the descent. He felt the lyrics '…this is serious' summed up the situation. Could he escort us to safety unscathed? It was a serious niggle. Thank goodness we couldn't mind read albeit we knew the situation was precarious.

There was packing to be done. I have no idea how anybody found their belongings. There were items we had left at base camp, items the porters had brought down for us, and the contents already in our rucksacks; it was a free for all. Marrying up the crampons, when three of us had exactly the same make, was pot luck. They were about the only pieces of equipment we didn't tag at the start of the expedition.

Before we left, the porters lit a bonfire. Martin insisted on the bonfire to dispose of our rubbish in a responsible manner. At last, the bag of full nappy sacks that had gone everywhere with us was disposed of. At least the snowball toilet paper had reduced the quantity of rubbish.

I soon became blasé about the condition of the roads as we headed back to Lachung and the Victoria Hotel, although Anita and Lynne might have had a different opinion! There was a little entertainment when our other vehicle became lodged on a rock. It was unquestionably jammed and required all hands on deck to lift it off its perch.

We arrived safely back in Lachung without further incident and found we'd been upgraded to a far nicer room. Was it that, or was it relative to where we'd just been? No, our room was much better –and Anita and Lynne were allowed a bottle of beer each! I had my Breezers and the odd tot of whisky to keep me happy.

Saturday 13th October – Lachung-Gangtok

IT WAS HEAVEN to visit the loo without having to put boots on. You realise very quickly how the simple things in life make all the difference. Cups of tea were brought to us in bed and, lesson learned, I bagged the bucket shower first. We still had no useful towel but plenty of clothes that would serve the same purpose.

It was a glorious morning and the first time we'd had proper views of the surrounding countryside. Pine trees, tiny waterfalls cascading down the steep terraced slopes; even the peaks came out of hiding and acknowledged our presence. The local cow walked by, presumably returning from her night out in Lachung.

We sampled the delights of the infamous road to Gangtok again but it was positively relaxing; there was no rain and a dry road surface made for easy going. Now we could appreciate just how much damage had been inflicted on the road and see more clearly where huge chunks had been washed away. I found it hard to believe how we'd got through in the atrocious conditions we had encountered.

We talked about the seat-belt business and what strategy would have been best. As you know, our driver put his seat belt on but nobody else in our car did. My thought was that if we went over the edge it would be fatal, and I would rather die sooner than later in that situation. The other theory was to leave your belt off so you might be able to jump out of the vehicle before you plunged to your death. As I was sitting in the middle of the back seat, there was fat chance that I could jump to safety. This was of no relevance now because we could clearly see the gaps to avoid, but it would be an interesting road to travel at night when many vehicles had missing headlights. Perhaps another time?

In case we'd forgotten what a monastery looked like, we visited another one. I thought this was the nicest of them all and the diversion broke the journey. They had the decorators in painting an intricate pattern on a ceiling. It was fascinating observing their skill and they were more than happy to let me watch. One spoke a little English and, once again, I tried to explain where I was from although I dropped the Geoffrey Boycott line.

A tiny puppy pottered about the grounds along with his mum. That was it: I made a beeline to have a chat with him. Hell, I'd just survived crevasses, glaciers and a road that beggared belief; I would risk rabies.

As we dropped into the outskirts of Gangtok, I finally switched my phone on. I hadn't missed contact with the outside world and, for a few moments when it started pinging as messages came in, I wasn't so sure about reading them. But why switch it on to then ignore it?

It was touching that friends seemed genuinely concerned for our welfare and eager to hear our news. I avoided the topic of summiting; that news would be broken when we were back in the UK. I wasn't quite ready for it yet. However, my thoughts on my technique remained the same: cut the crap and say it as it was. I wasn't good enough and it was too difficult for me. Life doesn't always go the way we want...

I was happily replying to various messages, knowing I'd bought a bolt-on deal for my phone. Later I discovered I should have read the small print. In my defence, I had enlisted a work colleague, someone half my age who understands these things far better than me, and he'd enabled the bolt-on. It transpired that India was excluded from the deal. Thank goodness I'd been out of range for most of our stay – I spent £150 in a handful of days! My work 'friend' did apologise afterwards. No wonder I'm a control freak: let go of the reins and look what happens. There is a happy ending; after pleading ignorance, senility and poverty, O2 refunded £90. Ten out of ten to their customer-service department.

Back at our hotel in Gangtok, we unpacked – then packed again for our internal flight the next day. People seemed to be very industrious, hanging items to dry before repacking. Sod that for a game of soldiers; what wasn't needed was stuffed wherever it would fit, whether it was wet, damp, muddy, clean or dry. Nothing would deteriorate because of another seventy-two hours of neglect. Laid back or lazy: you can decide on that one.

Sunday 14th October – Gangtok – Bagdogra – New Delhi

CONSIDERING WE HAD the comfort of a hotel bedroom, we didn't sleep that well. The noise from the road, and dogs continually barking throughout the night, tested even our sleeping pattern. Enjoying a proper shower and some clean clothes was bliss, however. A splash of perfume, a dab of eye shadow, and nobody would guess what I had been doing. I was also slimmer and for the first time in ages my trousers were too big for me. Unfortunately I knew that wouldn't last long.

Lynne missed out on breakfast, feeling less than well and relying on Imodium to help her on the long journey to Bagdogra airport. I felt for her. Carl seemed much better, except his leg was worse than when he'd first arrived. A few weeks later, he was told he required a hip replacement.

We allowed extra time for the drive to Bagdogra as we'd been warned that the road could be busier than usual. That was hard to imagine in view of the volume of traffic the day we arrived, but the information was correct. There was total gridlock on the narrow width of the road, trucks trying to pass one another and parked vehicles adding to the mayhem. I wondered if we'd miss our flight.

We were at a standstill long enough to get out of the car and stretch our legs. Street vendors were selling slices of water melon, which looked very tempting but I declined. Too risky. I had a bottle of Coca Cola with me so I stuck with that. It's something I rarely drink at home, but it's a handy alternative and supposedly good for the stomach, not that I was suffering.

After what seemed like an eternity, we were on the move again. I noted a car driving in the opposite direction, clearly a wealthy family with a modern car with an open sun-roof. A little girl was standing up in the car with her head stuck out of the sun-roof, hair blowing in the breeze, thoroughly enjoying her experience. My first reaction was one of horror at the potential danger, then my view altered slightly. Yes, it was dangerous, but have we gone too far the other way in the western world and been consumed by health and safety?

The once-muddy roads were now bone dry; a cloud of dust coated everything, reducing visibility. This time the feather duster was of no use.

I need not have worried about our flight and should have had faith in our new driver. He was determined we would not be late and, as we edged nearer the airport where the roads were less narrow, he used every scrap of available land. Only scooters and motorbikes had been undertaking on the dusty grass verges – but then there was us.

I was delighted and showed my appreciation by tapping him on the shoulder, giving him the thumbs up. Silly move on my part. Now he was out to impress and there was no stopping him. However, my adrenaline fix was overdue and it was time for more thrills; there had been few since leaving the glacier and I was suffering withdrawal symptoms.

There was a little entertainment at the airport, but not quite on the lines I was thinking of. Be careful what you wish for. For more than twenty years, Martin had been visiting India and taking camping gear through airport security. He kept some of the equipment with Mr Pandey in India to save taking it back and forth from the UK. There had been no problem on our incoming flight but now the authorities took a dislike to the camping stoves and insisted they would be confiscated.

Martin wasn't having any of it. Various bosses appeared but there was an impasse. According to our boss, a considerable amount of money was tied up in those stoves. According to the authorities, that was immaterial and they would not be going on the flight. What had been a busy airport when we arrived slowly became a ghost town as everyone, bar us, checked in and passed through security.

At the eleventh hour an agreement was reached whereby the airport would post the camping stoves to Mr Pandey in New Delhi. Surely the post then went by air, I asked myself. Either way, it was sorted.

It's hard to describe my feelings as we flew from Bagdogra to New Delhi. Mellow, perhaps; reflective most definitely, and a certain numbness. My ability had let me down but I was pleased that I hadn't broken my promise made back in March. I remained positive.

Martin beckoned me over to his seat on the plane. There, in the distance, was a golden glow and an outline of the Everest ranges. The height they were at, I could have easily mistaken them for clouds. I was thrilled. When I'd sent a wish list to Martin about our Himalaya trip all those months ago, I'd said I would like to see Everest but I was told that wouldn't be possible in view of our location. It was good of Martin to remember my wish.

Back in New Delhi, we were en route to the rather nice Metropolitan Spa Hotel and a style of driving that didn't even register on the 'thrillometer'. Having said that, the beautiful decor and lavish furnishings of the hotel did register on the 'pamper-yourself-ometer'.

After a quick room inspection, Dave and I went back downstairs. We were under the impression we were all meeting up within ten minutes. Fifteen minutes later, and with no sign of anybody else, we headed for the bar. We felt sure they would track us down.

Ah, they had heard of tonic water in India. A perfect G&T arrived on a tray with accompanying nibbles, served by an immaculately dressed waiter. The price they were charging was another matter, but what the hell?

Lynne was feeling slightly better and managed a bowl of soup. I was hungry but I wasn't letting down my guard, so much consideration went into my choice of food. I hadn't been ill and that was how I intended to remain. My mate the hand gel was still by my side.

Monday 15th October – New Delhi

IT WAS OUR last day in India. We had several hours before our flight at just before midnight, so it was an opportunity for some relaxation with modern comforts to hand. Morning coffee sitting by the pool in the shade of a parasol seemed all the more decadent after our expedition.

The women left the men behind and we headed for a shop within the hotel complex, a delightful establishment selling all manner of things. I don't think any of us could be regarded as shopaholics, other than when it comes to outdoor gear, but this was not your average shop and I could have easily spent more. Having little luggage space did the credit card big favours. Those who received a gift from me will know it weighed little and was compact. Apologies if it was not the perfect memento but it fitted in my luggage!

Martin went in search of the hotel manager and made a request that might not have sat well in such an establishment. Could he erect his tents within the hotel grounds? Not quite the image the hotel would like to portray, but a spot was found out of sight of the guests. Martin was handing his tents back to Mr Pandey's niece that evening and needed to dry them out.

Dave needed a barbershop that was located in a market close to our hotel. Within seconds of leaving the confines of the hotel grounds, we were approached by a very polite man asking if we needed help. Immediately I was on my guard, but he knew where the barbers were and offered to show us the way. On the basis of safety in numbers, we followed.

Carl stood guard outside the barbers, which was tucked down an alleyway. We planned to wait for Dave but the man's friend appeared. He could take us to a shop that might be of interest as Lynne had been looking for a scarf. It was agreed that Carl would wait for Dave and the first man would bring Dave and Carl to us. I hoped to goodness we were doing the right thing. I was anything but laid back and crevasses suddenly seemed far less of a worry.

Our escorts did as they said, and the men returned with Dave looking much tidier than when he went in, a little less like the wild man of Borneo – although more could have been taken off his beard. Communication was less than ideal and Dave had feared that the whole lot might disappear due to misunderstandings in translation.

Markets don't do it for me at the best of times; the hustle and bustle, along with the bartering, turn me cold. There was little pestering, but I was pleased to return to the hotel. After the many scarves Lynne was shown, she still couldn't decide if any were suitable!

A tour of New Delhi and 'Old' Delhi by air-conditioned minibus had been arranged for the afternoon. It's something I wouldn't repeat, but I'm not the ideal person to give an objective opinion. Sitting by the pool with some kind of aperitif in my hand would have been more than sufficient to keep me occupied.

Our time was drawing to a close, but not before an evening meal in New Delhi where we met Mr Pandey's niece, accompanied by one of Mr Pandey's high-altitude porters. A man of few words, he looked the real McCoy.

The excitement was nearly over – but not quite: the taxi to the restaurant was a ride in a tuk-tuk, a glorified bike with a small engine, a tiny seat and canopy. It was great fun in the traffic, with even less protection from the cars attacking you from all angles. It lit a temporary spark in my now fast-fading enthusiasm. I was sad, a little weary, but most of all I yearned to be home in Hellifield and back in the Yorkshire Dales.

Tuesday 16th October – And just when you think it's over...

IT WAS A bitter-sweet feeling as we landed at Leeds-Bradford Airport. It was good to be back in familiar surroundings, and yet I had an emptiness deep inside. Of course I felt tired, and I knew it would take several days before any form of normality re-entered my life, but I knew it would also take some adjustment to go back into the modern world.

How civilised the traffic was on the A65. There was no overtaking on blind bends, certainly nothing you could ever regard as a pothole, and nobody utilised the other side of the carriageway or the grass verges when the traffic came to a halt. A section of the A59 is often closed due to unstable ground and fear of landslips, but they don't know the meaning of unstable. How boring. However, I felt lucky to be driving back to Hellifield and heading for the Yorkshire Dales rather than an inner city.

Dave and I had another trip to look forward to. In a few weeks' time, we would be spending some time in Northumberland with Karen and Damien. A stroll on an empty beach, wrapped up against the elements, seemed like a good antidote, and this was how Karen wanted to celebrate her sixtieth birthday. There would be no roughing it; we'd have champagne and cake amongst the sand dunes on a secret beach admiring the North Sea, and then back to a rather nice cottage with all mod cons.

Karen was oblivious to the cake, champagne, secret beach

and sand-dunes plan but I had an idea in my head which I felt would work. Just because one fantasy hadn't gone quite as I envisaged, that was no excuse to end a habit of a lifetime of hoping and dreaming.

In the meantime, it was back to work and my commute to Leeds. How many people on that packed train were as lucky as me? Staring out of the train window, I looked at the high-rise buildings and roadworks but what I saw were rickshaws, glaciers and unclimbed peaks, accompanied by the 'Song of Sikkim'. Not the most obvious choice of music to rekindle memories of the Himalaya, but it still worked.

My first task was to break the news of the missing summit, feeling a little embarrassed. There was some surprise until I explained more fully but my reasons seemed to be acceptable. I just hoped they hadn't come across as an excuse but I could hardly have made it any clearer when I said I wasn't good enough for the job in hand! My colleagues' main concern was if I'd enjoyed it, and they were eager to hear my stories.

Richard, the man who often took the brunt of my 'cold-turkey' moments, suggested that I should make notes before time started to eat away at the memories. He'd said the same during my Munro challenge. He had experienced Borneo in his younger days and found his notes became more precious with the passing of time because you can forget unforgettable moments.

Various friends appeared to be looking out for my wellbeing, wondering if or when I would go through expedition withdrawal. Fifteen months of excitement, with the script not quite as I had written, was now at an end and that would surely have repercussions if my track record was anything to go by. But the cold turkey never got a look in.

On Sunday 28th October, Dave went to make a cup of tea to bring back to bed. You can't beat a few home comforts. But on his return…

'Dave, I can't blink.'

'Don't be silly, of course you can.'

'No, I can't… Look!'

Sure enough, my left eye would blink but the right was wide open and sore. A look in the mirror confirmed there was no movement and then I noticed my mouth had drooped to one side. Oh, my goodness, this wasn't looking good; I needed knowledge and fast.

'Dave, I'm off to Google this business.' I didn't mention my mouth as he hadn't noticed the droop. Of course, my first thought was a stroke.

Surfing the internet proved very helpful. Bell's Palsy came up and seemed a perfect match for my symptoms. Panic over, I went back to bed and shared my diagnosis with Dave. I would phone the doctor the following day and make an appointment. Dave seemed keen to take action immediately. No: tomorrow would be fine and there was a more pressing matter of meeting some friends for coffee.

I soon discovered that drinking my coffee was a little tricky with a wonky mouth; it appeared the droop was getting worse. As we said our farewells, Pat and Bill suggested a visit to the hospital might be a good idea. I said I'd think about it. However, back home there were chores to do. Quite uninteresting, but I could cope with a few mundane tasks and there were emails I needed to send before enjoying a well-earned glass of wine.

Too many people seem to enjoy an outing to their local A&E department. I had read that Bell's Palsy was a temporary paralysis of the face due to inflammation of the seventh cranial nerve. In time I would recover. There was no need to read any further; I had a general idea.

I'd liked the thought of becoming a doctor during my school days; I loved human biology but the grey matter did not stretch to such aspirations. The nearest I came was becoming a qualified embalmer when I worked in the funeral service. I still know where a carotid artery is, external, internal or just bog-basic common carotid.

I was just pondering on the merits of using a straw to drink my wine rather than struggling with a glass when the telephone rang. Another friend called Susan.

'Sue, I've just read your email. Okay about meeting up, but what's all this about Bell's Palsy?'

I went through the story and was told that I needed medical attention sooner rather than later. Susan's husband had suffered from Bell's Palsy many years earlier and had been told the sooner he started a course of steroids, the better the prognosis of a full recovery. Ah; I should have read the article thoroughly when I first Googled.

I came off the phone still wondering what I should do. Surely a few hours wouldn't make such a difference? Dave was becoming agitated at my obstinance. Okay, I would dial the 111 NHS helpline but I would speak to them myself; I didn't want Dave over-reacting and exaggerating my symptoms.

I'd heard mixed stories about the efficiency of this service, but credit where credit's due: they were excellent. Please do this, do that. I also discovered I could not smile nor could I raise my right eyebrow. 'No, Susan, you are not wasting our time and we want you to see a doctor this evening.'

The first port of call was our local hospital to see a GP under the out of hours' service. This was a stroke of luck; Skipton is only ten miles away and would avoid an A&E visit.

A doctor greeted us and we went through the same carry on, same questions. He felt sure it was Bell's Palsy but mentioned a variation called Ramsay Hunt Syndrome. The bottom line was not what I wanted to hear. He gave me a letter and I was on my way to A&E after all. For good measure, our nearest A&E,

only a few miles further on, might not be the most efficient option so we had to head to Bradford Royal Infirmary which was better suited to my problem. Things were going downhill by the minute!

Dave was relieved but the same could not be said for me, even though I'm not a person who suffers from 'white-coat' syndrome or a fear of hospitals.

I protested all the way there but my words fell on stony ground. We were lucky to find a pay-and-display parking space close to A&E. Dave dislikes automated systems and machines at the best of times, especially when asked to key in a car registration that he can't remember, so he asked me to tackle the machine. No, I wasn't going to buy a ticket because I wasn't going into the hospital.

Dave noted Wobble's registration, returned to the machine and bought the ticket himself. Then he told me that if he had to drag me in kicking and screaming then so be it. Thankfully that wasn't necessary. I was pleasantly surprised when the lady behind the desk seemed to know what she was talking about and asked me to take a seat.

The waiting time showing was four hours. It could have been worse and Dave had gone prepared. He felt we might be away for some time so, before leaving home, had thrown together some provisions: a drink and a few nibbles including an unopened bag of nuts.

Within fifteen minutes I'd gone through the triage process. The staff nurse was very pleasant and I was suitably impressed with him. Slowly I was coming to terms with my situation, and the people in the waiting area appeared to be quite civilised. You hear horrendous stories of fights and drunks and goodness knows what else in such places but it was a Sunday evening. I find it rather peculiar that the world and his wife accompany some patients to hospital. I understand having somebody there for moral support, and even bringing children if there is no alternative, but other than that I just don't understand it.

Dave was getting peckish so out came the picnic, but sadly he chose the bag of nuts. They had obviously been sealed extremely well because he struggled to open them. Normally this would not be cause for concern but, after a few attempts, I became increasingly worried. If Dave continued with his present strategy I could picture the whole waiting area peppered with nuts. He ignored my suggestion to select something else out of his goodie bag and thankfully the nuts were opened without incident.

A little more twiddling of thumbs and then two gentlemen arrived. The staff appeared to know them and I suspected there might be a problem, though I never anticipated what was about to happen. The older man headed towards a hand-gel dispenser. I saw him squeeze some gel into a plastic cup. Were my eyes deceiving me? A lady sitting near to the man kindly explained what the gel actually was. He proceeded to drink it, saying it was cheaper than alcohol! I have since learned that this can be quite normal.

At last my name was called. I asked the doctor if my husband could accompany me. She seemed surprised at my query but I wondered if relatives would be a hindrance in the cubicle. Of course, Dave could stay.

I was worried I wouldn't remember everything I was told. You think you're listening but somehow information doesn't always register. Yet again I rattled off the story. She confirmed Bell's Palsy and the urgency of starting a course of steroids. She asked if I'd recently suffered stress or trauma. I said no; I was quite happy. At this point Mr Pugh metaphorically fell off his chair laughing and strongly suggested I told the doctor the truth. Had I forgotten the Himalaya?

'Well, we have been to the Himalaya but I enjoyed it. I wasn't stressed.'

Dave stared at me in disbelief. The doctor explained that the medical profession was unsure what triggers Bell's Palsy. There are two theories: there could be a connection with a virus, or stress could play a part. I vote for the viral theory and I still say I wasn't stressed – I was the calmest of everybody on our trek. Anyway, I left the hospital with three types of eye drops, a boatload of steroids, anti-viral tablets and a drug to prevent stomach problems because of the steroids. Lastly, a roll of tape in order for me to tape my eye closed at night.

As we headed for the car, I ate a large slice of humble pie. I could not fault the hospital; they were marvellous. We passed some ambulances in the parking bays and I noted that the area had changed considerably since the last time I'd been there. But that was a very long time ago, when I was sitting in the front of an ambulance as traffic pulled over when we swung into A&E. Now that *was* an emergency; nobody was wasting anybody's time that day.

I spent the next few days improving my eating and drinking skills. Everyday tasks that I took for granted became an effort. I relish a challenge but learning how to drink a G&T without spilling it was not what I had in mind, and taking nineteen tablets was hardly a highlight of my day.

When I'd asked how long before normal service would resume, they had been loath to say. How long's a piece of string? Roughly speaking, I was looking at least six months. I was thinking on the lines of six days or, worst-case scenario, six weeks! Talking of 'roughly speaking', the letters B and P are the trickiest to pronounce when you have Bell's Palsy. Somebody had a wicked sense of humour naming this ailment. And when your surname is Pugh...

Every cloud has a silver lining. Thank goodness it didn't happen in the Himalaya and we had Northumberland to look forward to. What better timing for a relaxing break?

Remember Damien, the caring and considerate man who was there for me at the Matterhorn? This self-same man, now in Craster, who showed equal concern for my welfare. Now he reverted to his usual style when expressing love and compassion. It was the first time he had seen me since the Bell's Palsy business. It had only been a week and I was hardly looking my best. Within seconds of seeing me, I received a hug followed by an impromptu exaggerated mimic of my symptoms: one eye wide open, mouth askew and speaking with a slur. Oh, and a limp was thrown in for good measure. Cheeky – there was nothing wrong with my leg!

It was hilarious, but poor Karen was mortified at his black humour. Of course, that made the situation even funnier. I assured her that his therapy was the best I could have wished for; he knew me well enough to realise that I wouldn't be offended. It became part of the holiday and, when I was forced to wear a patch over my eye (not being able to blink meant any breeze or wind was painful), I was asked where my parrot was followed by an impersonation of Long John Silver. I still chuckle at those happy moments.

I've been asked several times if I would consider another Himalaya expedition in the light of what I know now. Without hesitation, the answer is yes. Even with all the uncertainties and unknown factors that go with the territory, I wouldn't want it any other way. Who knows, I still might get to summit a Himalaya peak.

Well, folks, that's where the story ends. I wondered where my next challenge would take me after the Himalaya and this book is it; you have just read it. It has rekindled many memories and emotions. Now, it's back to chasing rainbows.

If you are curious whether Karen had champagne and cake amongst the sand-dunes on a secret beach, admiring the sea –

yes, she did. Occasionally daydreams become reality. The next time you see a rainbow, please stop and think awhile. There may not be a pot of gold waiting for you but perhaps something far more precious.

Keep dreaming.

Sadly, our guide Martin Moran, lost his life in a climbing accident in the Himalaya, May 2019.

Acknowledgement

When it comes to expressing my thanks, I'll avoid writing a long list of names – but you know who you are! I have known some of you for more than fifty-five years, others are newcomers to my life, but you are all special people. You've offered encouragement, advice (if you could get me to listen!) and supported me in my challenges, including writing this book.

Life is full of uncertainties and that makes experiences and memories all the more precious. Sometimes bad luck can lead to good fortune; I could never have imagined in my wildest dreams the happiness I've experienced. But nothing would have been fulfilling had I not had people to support me and share both my delights and occasional disappointments.

So, no list of names – except for Dave, my dear husband. I really don't know how he has coped with me at times but I like to think our relationship and our adventures are as special to him as they are to me.

Thank you, everyone. There will always be a place for each of you in my heart.

In fond remembrance of Martin Moran; a very special person.